The CLOUD
NOTEBOOK

Ada Smailbegović

The Cloud Notebook © 2023 Ada Smailbegović

All rights reserved.

ISBN: 978-1-933959-61-0

Cover images by Tiziana La Melia, *Lake Moods (dome)*, 2013, gouache and watercolour on linen, approx 18 x 24 in. Documentation by Natasha Katedralis.

Design and typesetting by Mark Addison Smith.

Litmus Press is a program of Ether Sea Projects, Inc., a 501(c)(3) non-profit literature and arts organization.

Litmus Press publications are made possible by the New York State Council on the Arts with support from Governor Kathy Hochul and the New York State Legislature. This project is also supported in part by an award from the National Endowment for the Arts. Additional support for Litmus Press comes from the Leslie Scalapino–O Books Fund, The Post-Apollo Press, individual members and donors. All contributions are fully tax-deductible.

LITMUS PRESS
925 Bergen Street #405
Brooklyn, New York 11238
litmuspress.org

SMALL PRESS DISTRIBUTION
1341 Seventh Street
Berkeley, California 94710
spdbooks.org

Cataloging-in-publication data is available from the Library of Congress.

The CLOUD NOTEBOOK

Ada Smailbegović

to Azra and Braco and the cats left behind in the time of war

You recognize the person in territory, though she is not seen, like space around the statue, as if complexity hidden from us would be revealed, invisible as the yellow back of a lizard on sand and visible as its dark claw.

—Mei-mei Berssenbrugge, ***Four Year Old Girl***

...it is more that we only notice the arrival of those who appear "out of place." Those who are "in place" also must arrive; they must get "here," but their arrival is more easily forgotten, or is not even noticed.

—Sara Ahmed, ***Queer Phenomenology***

For it is exceeding difficult in some objects, to distinguish between a prominency and a depression, between a shadow and a black stain, or a reflection and a whiteness in the color. Besides, the transparency of most objects renders them yet much more difficult than if they were opacious.

A sheet stretched across a wooden frame in one kind of light appears almost like a lattice drilled through with abundance of small holes. In the sunshine it looks like a surface covered with golden nails; in another posture, like a surface covered with pyramids; in another with cones; and in other postures of quite other shapes.

In a blue envelope a figure places an object whose edge we cannot know and which does not have parts but is more of a collapsed soft form.

A figure in a scene is someone although they do not look like themselves, as when lit by circumstance another's face closes in change, the marble left in sheets in sunlight.

A tent appears: it is white, a single stretched sheet on the open surface of the field—the field itself is full of mirrors that replicate the strands of grass, doubling them and then doubling them again, and so it is a site of mimesis.

She says, "everything in a landscape is as important as everything else."

She says, "quote the voices of others in this way."

Sometimes inside the cover of the tent she holds the ears of rabbits close to her face, holds them in her hands, places their paws in her mouth.

"Sensation is matter touching itself," she thinks.

"There is even this shot in the film: snow falling in the summer and white foam floating down the river."

"To gather dispossessed feelings in common," at night she moves the green bed.

Years later, at night, she will move the sheets off her bed sliding them in one continuous take onto the floor and dragging them into the hallway where she will sleep.

Instead of a tent, she makes a lake with the black surface of her coat on the ground.

Another tent is made out of gauze and stretched all the way out to the exit of the sea.

At its most dilated, memory resides in the upper echelons of the sky and enters the present without instrument.

Can a sky or a shape that moves at another pace or rhythm be a kind of memorial for another that moves at a pace yet faster or slower than itself?

Or can the appearance of something occurring against the blue wall of a dimly lit room be a parallel to the appearance of the sky and its occurrence?

The objects fall into distinct rhythms and this is what causes one small part of the object to appear as a pink tent—it begins pointing and in another area it turns into a field of squiggly white lines, which move wormlike across its surface.

One side of the tent opens, it is like a long red sheet that pulls away to reveal the crevice, not anything visible but just a sense of an interior.

She draws a picture of chaos. It is made of red berries or strings of rope or the possibility of red berries must exist somewhere within it. A bird sits on top of chaos. She has made a tiny raft on which she positions a small pile of red berries, in the opposite corner of the raft she makes a small pile of deer dung. This has happened some time ago so there are now thin white threads sprouting out of the surface of the dung, visible there as hairs touching the color of the sky.

He says, "I dedicate this to the space between the new leaves and where the old leaves used to be."

She says, "notice the spaces between a bird's flights and perchings, where a cut in one shape reveals something else in the other."

She wraps paper around an object then, a piece of bread that someone will carry into the dust of the world.

The world is moving already then, within a smooth pink surface another cut occurs impressing a pink oval.

A song is playing.

She buys a pink notebook. On each of its pages a shape of a different cloud, so that in moving the pages in a certain way one can feel the rhythm of the moving sky.

Again she sits to write the history of all liquids, the oils pressed out of the seeds of plants, lymph, the waters of various lakes and seas.

In the invisible room the women wear pink jumpsuits, they touch the creams, foams and froths, rub circles of color onto the flat surfaces of things, make marks within squares on small pieces of paper with pencil, they pull tubes of cloud paint out of clear plastic bins and place them into the pink Ziploc pouches lined in bubble wrap. "The feeling before and after purchasing something is the most delicate feeling," she reads in a blue book, the color of a particular kind of egg.

△   △
△   △

The blocks of cement are striped with peach stripes.

They sit on the grass in dresses and the deer come to leap between them.

Below is a small lake or a stream.

She makes a sheet of gold squares.

Within its folds everything begins to occur.

Your body disappearing the way a landscape disappears beneath the morning, the spaces between the trees, the white flowers appearing far away in time rather than space, becoming a stain of color in the unrisen mist—it is here that your mouth disappears, the white plastic bag moves softly over the grass, something is held and then released.

Before you disappear she takes a photograph of the circle of the woods, the contours of a blue metal pyramid divided within them. Or on the wall someone has cut the shapes of constellations and the light presses out through the tiny holes.

So she made the cuts in the floor to make the surface of the moving river appear visible through them.

Or a long piece of wood rises with the tide and is left on the rocks to make a seesaw.

Within this interval of time you disappear.

In the film the water is a second medium; it moves the wet tissues along the slick surface of the metal, reanimating them so that we cannot tell the difference between these two moments.

The men who gather things in the grass wear yellow reflective vests.

You are wearing one of these too.

The lines of blue rope tied between the trees in the yard.

She writes in her cloud notebook: "Emotions are the only way of having the world repeat itself."

She writes in her cloud notebook: "The lining of the world is supple soft. A snail has secreted a thin sheath of slime around itself. This is written on a blue piece of paper."

The milieu of the body is an outside that is more specific than the outside outside.

The body draws a rectangle within which something felted can appear on the surfaces of things, or it makes signs in the thin liquids that drape over the surfaces of slower, more solid forms.

When describing the last movements of something, the resolution of description changes: A small armadillo wanders onto the road again, the white flowers appear as a scrim in the grass, an old woman changes size, a white mouse chews on a plant in the night, they go on a road trip to look for seashells, the sky opens between them, she imagines blocks of time within which actions will occur.

That time between knowing and thinking.

She replaces all feelings toward objects with more indirect smaller objects toward which feelings can occur. In this way, the world becomes controllable, like a set of colored pebbles, but it also is not, or things still move in the world independently of their extrinsic causes: "If you had left the water camp the day after the day you left, if I had not touched your mouth on the motel bed in Connecticut, if I had not written about the moon rising above a baseball field in the mountains etc., you would not have been in that place at that time." This is a problem of narrative.

"There is no other possible world," he says, "otherwise there would be another possible universe beside this one, and then another, or there would be an outside to substance, which would then have to be another substance breaking with the first, and then another, the planet would have to have a face facing outward," the door closes between them.

Beneath this is a boundary that is impassable to language.

The conversation ends.

A small boat floats in an even smaller lake.

She lies in the gravel parking lot to look at the sky again where they had touched the small pebbles with their feet.

It is from that vantage point that nothing appears in the sky: it is like a blue door.

She says, "gather everything in the surface of your hand."

She writes in her cloud notebook: "The red shapes disappear in the water like planets."

$$\underline{\triangle \quad \triangle}$$
$$\underline{\triangle \quad \triangle}$$

Such is the contact between thought and the world that to think of the taste of an oyster one must have tasted an oyster at some point.

She sees that the ceiling has collapsed or is collapsing.

The color of the sky attaches to the external thing that is the color of the sky.

She writes in her cloud notebook: "The sensation 'blue' becomes the 'blueness' of the sky, the sensation 'green' becomes the 'greenness' of the lawn, and so forth. We recognize the sky by the feature 'blue' and the lawn by the feature 'green.'"

A tent is just a provisional structure made out of sticks on the surface of the sea.

The forces of the sea allow some atoms to turn in color from a closed blue to the open sheets of marble luster.

In this scene her blood is drawn, or a liquid, perhaps ink, is pierced into her skin.

She transfers a small amount of a pink cream onto her hand.

You pass a broken wooden comb through your hair.

The cloud notebook has appeared like a character in things.

On the floor of her workplace she finds a live mouse stuck on a piece of white paper covered with glue. Now she is ungluing it softly by wetting its fur and moving drops of water between it, her fingers, and a small pink bowl of water. She will later release it behind a small bush.

She thinks of a painting like those painted by Bosch of the underworld where blue insects are fucking one another or they are not entirely insects, their underbellies revealing the wet, soft flesh of humans. In another corner, two or three have gathered around a fire rising out of and within the upright sticks that have been positioned and pierced into the ground.

Every occurrence arises out of every possible occurrence.

Or causality is a matter of indirection.

Sometimes she dreams of an apparatus, an empty glass box that can be positioned in front of a window, into which a fragment of the world could likewise be positioned to ascertain the asymmetries in its patterns of causation.

Or inside her mouth something moves, an entire new world appearing out of the soft sounds.

She writes in her cloud notebook: "A whole world can arise out of the random movement of atoms as they bump into one another and come to make shapes, the shapes of which then come apart also; the same way an entire world can emerge out of the recombination of the letters of the alphabet as they touch one another."

And so what is visible or sensible may reveal the mark of something that is hidden.

She says, "I have not seen it appear in this way, with this pattern of unevenness or with this set of uneven shadows, all of them still blue, for instance."

Or this painting is a vast beach, only this beach is a recreation and so each of its sand grains is countable, all of them countable into a sum.

She thinks of countable nouns and those that make a kind of pile or cannot be resolved into grains, like grains of milk for instance.

On the floor of the room only a mattress and a large bag of sugar out of which she is taking spoonfuls with a silver spoon. "This is a form of soft food," she thinks. Not capturing the birds that are sitting in the trees, nor the pods of fruit, nor the porcupine that has hid in the ground.

"Sensation is infinitely divisible, even if matter itself is not," he says, "and so while a wave cannot be cut into a thousand tiny waves, the sound of a wave is a summation of the sounds made by a thousand waves."

She has attempted to make a changing thing, something appearing as an infinite unfolding as it is touched by the world, and yet one way that it is touched stops it, and now it can no longer move or be touched again.

She waits there in the water, and sometimes speaks at the sky. It is in this way that speech becomes indirect or indirectly addressed.

The objects appearing as dots of paint without a mood.

And so, a winter scene in the Maine woods is present here, but appears grammatically hypothetical with hollows between what composes it.

All of the objects are left folded. They appear as an end. But this is not because an end is known or anticipated, only that an end appears within each day as an occlusion.

"I wish to go to the docks," she says, "or be left dissolute."

△   △

△   △

She wraps pink quartz crystals into sheets of bubble wrap, rolls a sponge stained softly with semen into a cylinder and ties it together on separate occasions with six strings of red wool to hold it away from unfolding into a flatness.

In this tiny performance she has bled into the middle of her bed, and so they stand there with wet sheets, using the wetness to pull one kind of liquid out of another.

We have entered the sky she thinks, and now we can see the clouds. This week she has entered the sky on five distinct occasions.

"Different countries proportion the geometries of their fields differently," she observes.

"The money has appeared and then disappeared," she thinks.

One day she realizes that she too can look.

Although the objects appear so different to her from across the room than when she has grasped them.

The body of a bee is fuzzy and striped and yellow and black.

A man named Sparrow laughs.

Sometimes she thinks she hears his laugh even when he is not present, at airports for instance.

She hides the large red bowl in the closet so no one can use it, but she cannot find the small spoon.

One year she enters a bed in a snowstorm.

Another, she hides in the pink folds of it after an event.

She asks the person on the other side of the phone if they could arrange to hold something.

The grace of the trees is yellow, this thing when repeated is like a film they saw once. The bodies of the people in the film had to walk around on their knees and eat shit. The shit was really chocolate.

She has tears in her eyes.

Once in Chinatown she held onto a plant on the sidewalk.

△   △
  △   △

One tent is made out of a fabric, which itself is covered in feathers, another out of a fabric made of mutated insects, one orange with a plump, inflated wing, asymmetrical with the other, one green with pink dots interspersed on its abdomen unevenly, one with a swallow left eye.

This one is made out of the sea, or a green blanket, which may be the color of the sea, golden hairs and yellow wallpaper. Inside the tent you can hear the sounds of seabirds.

This tent is a tunnel dug underneath the tarmac of an airport.

This tent is made out of white rocks.

This tent is made out of pink foam. The foam has been squirted into a pile, the shape of a cake with a flat top within which they make a cavity, the tent is somewhere inside of that cavity.

This tent is resting inside the shell of a blue egg.

This one is like a camera that a reindeer has entered into. It moves on the ground of its inner surface. Sometimes it is seen moving from the side, its legs making an inner shape as they appear to touch in midair. Or, we see its rump and white tail, the antlers moving elsewhere like lines in the middle distance.

If lit correctly, even a solid wall can appear as an opening. There is no allegory.

Think of these tents as a tiny space of projection or a tiny screen on which anything can be depicted or anything can happen. This screen may be held in your hand, but it is just a wrapping of gauze or fabric in which colors are appearing.

The visibility of small figures moving through a grid of space.

She seems to stand in a landscape covered with dunes of snow, in front of a doorway.

In this scene, they throw rocks wrapped in cloth in order to find the passage to the future. Only the future is hidden in one balancing stick of wood positioned by the receding water into the crevice of the rock.

She writes in her cloud notebook: "When the plum passes out of the sepia toned world."

She writes in her cloud notebook: "Instead, he disassembles the bomb and scatters its pieces. Rain begins to fall into the room through its ruined ceiling."

She sees a white sailboat moving on the red cover of a book.

The duck that she stole from the park pond and left on the couch moves across the balcony railing to the neighbor's apartment and is discovered several hours later in an identical position on the neighbor's couch.

One day in the woods she finds a raccoon skeleton and brings it home. Only it is not her home but someone else's home that she is subletting off Craigslist. She forgets the raccoon skeleton there and has to call a month later to ask: "Hello, did you happen to find a raccoon skeleton in your house?" The woman on the other line says "No."

She writes in her cloud notebook: "She has beautiful laughter as we eat the cookie dough. The bear as it lowers its body into the water of a lake has round hips like a woman."

One day she picks a decorative cabbage out of a planter in front of an expensive restaurant and eats it, the cabbage is purple and bitter.

The affinity of night enters her then.

△   △

△   △

At the edge of the park where she makes a cut toward the beach one could say that the park is rimmed by the night or rimmed by the sea.

She writes in her cloud notebook: "All cloth is rimmed in the white lace of the sea. The light spills from the street lamps onto the highway. There is no afterwards."

One day she goes to a party at a rich house in the mountains. She climbs in a bush and makes out with someone. She is drinking peach coolers and so tastes of fake peaches. After that her name becomes "Peaches" or her name becomes "Leopardprint" or her name becomes "Waterfall" or "Misaligned."

She thinks about whether she wants to stretch her desire into language, or if it is language that is the thing stretching here, the yellow caterpillars hanging from the beams of a pink house on white threads.

Inside the pink house, small cut-out black and white pictures from a magazine of communist sculptures: women working, carrying wheat, bearing children, in uniform.

When playing trivia, she always considers Laika, the dog that was sent to space. This is never the answer, but it is the first fact she knew and so it seems to stand for what is factual, what is real.

She writes in her cloud notebook: "Delicate empiricism occurs when unlike things encounter one another. The forests of May are so thick. They have positioned the neon sheet of orange paper testifying to sanitation standards next to a light pink bottle of rosé."

△   △
 △   △

Think of each of these surfaces as a tiny theatre.

One could project their feelings onto the surface of the birch bark; that is, one could watch tiny movies on the surface of the birch bark in the same manner that one could otherwise use a sheet that is stretched between the trees.

She writes in her cloud notebook: "Use the image of the geometric solid surrounded by the forest."

She writes in her cloud notebook: "How difficult it is to describe something invisible like that, and yet so solid and tangible when it is present."

The residues of someone else's movements or actions that are recorded in how objects are folded, how plants are left.

After steaming milk all day she dreams of steaming milk all night.

She makes a spiral movement with the finger of one hand in the air in order to mimic the movement of water as it eddies, or moves backwards in time or space.

She gathers all of the hairs out of the blanket and puts them into an envelope—a green envelope / the color of the inside of a green apple, or a little greener, a cold green then. This is as much of him as there is left on earth. The hairs look live, golden, tenuous.

She writes in her cloud notebook: "The roof of the convent on which there is a tennis court and plastic flowers. The curve of his bike on that steep street where the horse used to leap."

She thinks of finishing a task or not being able to get through it, as though a task were a block of ice.

In the meantime, they had lined up all the limes into a pyramid, then all the apples into a heap.

The ants are crawling somewhere very small on a windowsill overlooking a park full of snow. There is a pot of instant tomato soup on the stove being mixed with a wooden spoon. The container of milk has a perfect representation of a mountain on it. The mountain is blue. One day the trees in the park will be cut for firewood. It will be a time of war that is invisible at this moment. This moment from which we are looking.

$$\underline{\triangle \quad \triangle}$$
$$\underline{\triangle \quad \triangle}$$

Throwing your body against the aquamarine floor is almost like throwing your body against a body of water.

They are carried to one edge and then passed onto another.

This is not only abstract, a border may be crossed: one conveys one to another.

It is winter in this scene.

When the event is too big to fit into a story, we cannot see the causalities attached to its duration.

A body moves until it is touched by another body, upon which it may change its course, stop, or begin moving faster.

She writes in her cloud notebook: "Create a loose weaving as though with thick colored straw. One liquid can pass out of a tincture of another. The golden straws of nostalgia look backwards even as the movement is opening out, and yet this is what makes the moment distinct, able to proliferate through its imaginings."

You do not exist anymore.

Nor all of the motel pictures of waterfalls you would have seen.

The soft orange sheets are just a carrier, they can carry the trace of the other for a while into the distance: terrycloth or green compressed bags, a wooden bowl, the claws of a German Shepard on the wooden floor.

She writes in her cloud notebook: "The German Shepard moves between the trees in this story. He feels guilty for looking a little too long at the other two kissing."

She is shown to put the objects into tightly sealed Ziploc bags. The others have discovered this without knowing, the way that one walks to a bathroom at night in the dark in a strange house.

We look for the lizards, for the acorns, but they cannot be seen.

Nothing mills out or crawls out to sun itself on the steps.

One day she will receive a Ziploc bag the color of the sun.

△   △

△   △

In the middle of the movie a cut occurs, but this cut is not shown, and so it is not clear how the two sides of the movie touch one another, the off-ramp and the on-ramp do not align.

She writes in her cloud notebook: "The common sunstar is found on rocky bottoms, coarse sand and gravel. Very small sunstars are sometimes found in rock pools."

She writes in her cloud notebook: "It is reddish on top with concentric bands of white, pink, yellow, or dark red. It is white on the underside."

In this scene they are eating pancakes in a diner on New Year's Day.

She writes in her cloud notebook: "To have been shipped is to have been moved by others, with others. It is to feel at home with the homeless, at ease with the fugitive, at peace with the pursued, at rest with the ones who consent not to be one."

A wave of the sea rises onto the concrete platform and enters the tiny holes in her electronic objects. Why do all objects circle around their holes, like the way that a forest circles a clearing, or a wolf circles a rabbit? She remembers an early postcard that says "a thing is a hole in a thing it is not." The postcard had a picture of a cinderblock on it with a loaf of bread positioned in each of the holes. It was made by Bamby.

She cannot understand why sometimes or often some lose faith just before something changes. But the moment of change cannot be seen until one looks backwards, turns around halfway through a story or a game of hopscotch. The angel of history faces backwards into the storm.

She writes in her cloud notebook: "The birds fly through the sky, passing across where the pass has already occurred."

Someone stops by a body of water and looks across through to the fantasy occurring on the other shore. A yellow rope floats along in the water.

She says, "I am I because my little dog knows me."

But what if the dog in this story is also changing, she thinks.

If all the world were powdered up and placed into a device where it could be smelled, then this form of translation between species could occur.

She wakes up one morning and buys a cap covered in large colored dots.

The dots are of different sizes and some are overlapping.

Inside the color of the sea is another pattern and so we cannot say that all of the sea is of one color entirely.

A hedgehog sleeps all through the winter or a hedgehog sleeps all through the night, a tick can lie asleep for eighteen years, although can this be called sleep or is it really a space of waiting?

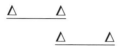

On the opposite shore she sees lines of lightning cutting through the sky, only sometimes they are not really cutting but rather make the sky come together at one singular point.

The legs of the table are yellow. In some other land there is a girl with yellow hair: these are the threads that are lost in the story and so nothing gathers them.

A set of glass marbles moves across skin, or moves across another surface, or one by one they sink into her mouth, or they sink into the sea.

The two figures move toward the mountains and buy plants: one magnolia tree, one hydrangea (blue) and one lilac tree.

The neighbor comes to mow her lawn at dawn while she is sleeping to remove her dandelions before they disperse into his yard.

She writes in her cloud notebook: "1. Weave something out of thick straw of different colors. 2. During war decide between feeding the tigers at the zoo or freeing them. 3. Consider the events that are outside of human occurrences within a historical moment. Such events may be historical. 4. Consider that the door may have been made under a different regime. 5. Write a tiny performance. 6. Think about the way that one talks about a slow unfolding / the actions like the removal of things."

There she finds herself around a small hole opening in the sky. Someone says: "As the whipping cream thickens, it begins to fold over itself or into itself. It is an object without a legible interior or exterior. Elements often move across a line into a new state, only sometimes that line may be more like an inlet or a space of waiting."

It demarcates the edge of where one surface begins and the other opens out or is left off.

As in an open mouth.

Then someone says, "either go to Owl Drugs or never go to Owl Drugs."

At night, as she walks, she circles it, this other invisible relation.

She writes in tiny sentences that cannot be held.

No one calls any more.

She writes in her cloud notebook: "When mosquitoes dance in the sunset, they do not see our big human sun, setting six kilometers away, but small mosquito suns that set about half a meter away. The moon and stars are absent from the sky of the mosquito."

△   △
 △   △

In this story the hedgehog does not survive.

She is hungry but she does not see this hunger as a quest.

Later, she will dream of the others, waiting in lines for water, cutting a large tree down on the edge of a soccer field in a group that is moving in a line to help lower its body down to the ground, running across any open space.

They will not appear on television, she hopes.

This will be relentless.

She will stop washing.

In this tiny performance she is swimming in an open sea or

the sea is not wide open or is near a rocky beach. She hears buzzing at the surface of the sea where a green beetle has fallen into the water. Its body is thick and metallic green. It takes the form of a forest that has been poured out of another material body. But can anything be said to be poured into the shape of one body out of another? Even liquids, when poured into a glass or a bowl or another receptacle, only assume its shape as a form of mimicry, and so of all metal when it is cast into a shape that represents the world. The beetle's black legs are treading water. They have tiny hooks on them so that they can grasp things or touch things at two points, or perhaps these are feelers for feeling the surface of the world. The world divides itself then. The beetle has fallen out of ordinary time. Its time now is inside a window, a narrowing within which few details are visible but those that are present fill the entire space of sensation.

She looks outside of her window and sees a pair of eyes. A tiny black kitten is sitting on the grass or is half hidden by the fronds of the palm tree.

She says, "this is an unaligned geometry, do not confuse it with the sea."

As the snail traverses its environment, it leaves the traces of the scales of its past traversals.

She writes in her cloud notebook: "There is no one physical scale that intrinsically is the scale of texture. As your plane circles over an airport, texture is what a whole acre of trees can provide. But when you're chopping wood, a single tree may constitute shape or structure within your visual field, whereas texture pertains to the level of the cross-grained fibers of the wood in relation to the sleek bite of the axe."

The error lies in obscuring the difference between life and representation, she thinks; she tries to breathe into the collapsing gap between them, inflating it.

It is a bit like how she imagines inflating a yellow safety life vest on an aircraft would feel, using a red tube.

She thinks of the face.

As she is watching fireflies one night, a large cat appears out of the woods and approaches her. The cat is larger than any she has seen and has tufts on its ears and so she knows the cat is not an ordinary cat. It stares at her as she is sitting on the porch and then leaps back into the woods without a word. A word would not be expected here.

In the kitchen she can smell cabbages but cannot see them. There are no cabbages or they may be invisible. She checks for openings between the walls. Checks if a family of cabbages may be living there.

Sitting at the edge of the sea but not within it, she sees a hundred silver bodies moving in concert. They must be able to sense one another with their skins even without touching, she thinks. Sometimes one or the other of them flashes as light catches it. This is a form of infinite cinema. Or, this is a form of cinema that does not diminish in detail.

The world is full of tiny screens, she thinks.

When human skin is touched, it records both the duration of touch, that is the interval that opens between the beginning and end of touch, as well as the discrete points at which contact occurs, but this interval also disappears or is not felt continuously.

She wants to wear a pink plastic thing, perhaps a bit like a beach ball.

Then one early Sunday morning there is a change of scene. She has entered a tiny hole.

The girls appear.

They are wearing transparent pantyhose and high-waisted black underwear. Some are also wearing leashes. Some cat ears. Or she may be mistaken. There may not be any cat ears in this scene.

She wants this thing that is made for them to be made for her.

She thinks about this as she is sucking on their pink claws, tearing their red antennae. As she looks around, everyone is sucking the liquids out of the heads. They have compound eyes, she thinks.

△   △

△   △

One could think of this cone as a salt shaker. The memories dusting out of its tip. Or perhaps it is more like a sky full of constellations, invisible from a well-lit street, appearing only as blankness or the unseen.

A woman comes down the aisle and hands her a warm wet napkin with a pair of tweezers.

It is released a moment too soon, and even though she catches it, there is an unsettled sense of it being in the air for too long.

The larvae come out of their red cocoons before the leaves appear.

Everything has fallen out of sync, she thinks.

Even the storm arrives later than expected and so the sideways wind opens one wing of a double window causing it to crash and break through another. When she returns late at night, she discovers shards of glass on the floor and small wet areas.

It feels as though one part of the world has broken through another.

She offers to pay for this transference, hoping to contain it.

There is a smell in the air of horses, as though horses were nearby.

The wind makes the same sound in the trees as it would in any clearing, in any woods.

The grid of stone positioned over the grass is identical everywhere. Or was the grid there initially, the grass appearing only afterwards. In this sense one could say it is more like a stone lace or a kind of loose foam than a true grid. And yet, each of its openings is a site of appearance or a hole. In one opening a small plant with toothed leaves. In another, a dandelion plant without a flower. In another, three stone eggs waiting for an invisible bird.

If one were to throw a wooden grid the size of a small window onto a seemingly empty field, something would appear in it.

That is to say that perhaps fields are not simply entirely empty.

At one point a black bird with white on the underside of its wings is seen rising from a field for instance.

She says, "jam can appear if a yellow plum tree casts its overripe fruits onto a stone platform by the sea."

The sea is not an actor in this scene.

△ △
△ △

She says, "a blue and white tarp sits on the grass."

This is happening by a woodpile.

When a fig is broken in half, it opens to a completely new color that could not be anticipated from the outside.

She presses it then through the thin metal grid of the fence until its meat drops through and can be reached by the chickens.

The ocean is simply a series of latches and dots moving through space, she thinks.

Or the voice makes an interiority, almost a whispering, and then the body sharply exteriorizes itself, becoming a figure walking on the grassy, green square of the park. On the outside, it participates in actions: eating ice cream from a cone, licking salt off a hand.

She thinks that she recognizes each of the bridges that she passes over from a video that she has seen. The blue metal that composes them is often shaped aerodynamically so that at times they look more like an airplane than an object that remains close to the ground.

As she glances down, she sees the tail of an animal detached by the side of the road. The rest of the animal is missing. The tail has stripes that circle it.

She thinks about all the animals that may be missing.

Uncertain whether the hedgehog that she sees may be the last hedgehog on earth or whether there is one more hiding somewhere in the woods.

Even though the woods are visible, they cannot be entirely searchable, entirely known.

Part of the reason is not a problem of visibility but the impossibility of being everywhere at once, as in one is always in a particular position making the observation and cannot be more than oneself or anywhere else.

Another way to say this is that even though one may consider the observer to be standing aside, outside the circumstances of the scene, she is nevertheless susceptible to being touched by the unfolding of the events.

The brittlestar sitting on the bottom may break itself into pieces creating a cluster of herself, each of the pieces possessing along its entire surface "an eye."

Within this apparatus, vision does not produce a tiny room on the insides of things, all of its shapes correspondent to the shapes on the outside of the world.

Rather, the world itself may appear as a pattern in the surface, as in the surface may shift shape to become the dots and circles and strands and rocks that surround it, and so it may become indistinguishable from the world, of it in a sense.

She asks then: "Will another world appear?"

The grid of appearance where this may occur being a tiny room on top of a building where a roof has been removed and so, sitting in the room, looking upward, one is entirely exposed to the surface of the sky.

Within a single rectangle anything may appear.

The shards of glass flickering as they catch the light and are then released by it in turn.

Inside the rectangle's milky green shape she sees several orange bodies emerging for an instant to touch the surface of the air.

Then, inside of what becomes the rectangle's gray surface she sees small pelts covered in grease, a plastic bottle, a swan, yellow foam.

△　　△
△　　△

She notices that the opposite shapes appear beneath and behind the branches of the trees. It is as if they make the seeing of what is behind them possible.

What appears as pressed color or chalk, the shade moving over a green door.

The streets lit in the circumstance of leaving.

A surprise something falls into, because a surprise may be an eruption of white on its stems.

Or there between the two lions she sleeps, or there where a pink lion is sleeping on the sidewalk she sits between it and the sky. She thinks of the crescent of the other's body now pressed into her finger.

Or when this body enters her hand, it is quicker than it seems.

Something towers above her then too, the shine of a blue pot in the detail of the world. Its entangled spirit, its appearance near the sky but not within it.

As they enter the water, the waves surprise them, and so they are forced to let go of the fine powder they are holding in their hands, this motion of letting it go almost as involuntary as a blink or a startle, one could not quite call it a decision.

Something negotiates or cuts across small blue ribs of surface.

The orbits of the world separate then, or it is as if a glassy surface appears between the worlds.

On each of its sides the shapes are discernible but not entirely visible, as if a scrim or a milky substance covers them, as if a breath exiting beneath a cold even sky clouds them over.

She cannot think then.

Someone near her says, "dogs eat placenta after they give birth, but I may buy my wife a ham sandwich."

She thinks of all of the objects that may take on the shades of burgundy or maroon that may find themselves side by side, on the same conceptual table.

He says, "red objects do not have discrete edges, when we see them as separate, we may only be imposing a cut where no cut necessarily appears between things."

She thinks of the relation that stained glass windows have to the surface of the world.

The surface of the water always surprises her.

In the night she walks near a yellow house with a white roof. On top of the roof there are solar panels and the trees near it have been trimmed so as to leave an open path to the sun. She cannot see whether the statue that had been propped up against one of the trees has been removed. The surface of the world remains oblique, closed to her.

Small patterns of stumps appear in the shiny water.

△   △

△   △

She says, "if it has disappeared we would not know it, not know if it has gone or is only missing."

Another hedgehog may still be running through the woods.

She passes by a moment where you ate the banana that had been lying on the sidewalk.

The sun is in things but so is the wind.

She does not know what is visible yet.

In a tiny pot a plant whose leaves are orbs.

Someone positions texts about objects on top of objects that they represent, a copy of Ponge's *La Table* on top of a table, for instance.

Or what occurs takes a different turn, a toy in the shape of a hedgehog being positioned on top of a book about hedgehogs by a small boy.

△ △

△ △

She writes in her cloud notebook: "When we first heard the sound in the morning, it sounded like a tea kettle or a coffee maker. We thought that the other one of us had woken up early to make coffee. Later we saw that the sound was coming from a breathing whale that we could see through the window. The window looked like a postcard but later we saw that the tiny waves were moving in it, so we thought it was a television."

On each of the windows a blue X.

One morning she buys a spider plant by the river to cleanse the air. She gives this spider plant to a person. Sometimes this person lies next to the spider plant pretending that they are lovers.

Sometimes I think about how you are not with the goats anymore and how in the story that you told me you were shoveling goat shit all winter until one day you discovered a goat dead underneath all the shit you were shoveling.

In the absence of a person all those who had touched and held the person, spoken to, looked at, listened to, felt the person, gather around a tree thinking about the person who is now invisible.

"Invisible?" you say.

"Yes."

$$\underline{\triangle \quad \triangle}$$
$$\underline{\triangle \quad \triangle}$$

She says, "I have nearly lost consciousness twice in relation to the same object, the last time in a desert, early morning, having fallen to the ground, my nylons ripping."

The golden glasses reappear in a dream, or they appear on another's face, or on the faces of several figures who do not know they are in a repetition together.

The desert then appears blue, having absorbed the interior of the body.

Or we see the desert in this moment non-representationally because all the events that are present—the fall to the ground, the scratches, the sound of the nylons ripping—do not add up to the event that is invisible.

This event seems to occur in a dimension that cannot appear on a sheet.

As one of its surfaces it acquires a pink marsh made up of something granular, tapioca pudding perhaps, and as this marsh expands, it begins to fold in on itself, gluing into a kind of dough, which begins to appear as a sphere, then on one part of it a bamboo forest begins to grow.

At night she sees an eye looking at her from a building across the street. The eye must be there in the daytime too, but she notices it only at night.

A small dog that passes by has a hot pink leash.

In a dream she walks past the house where she used to live. The pink triangle composed out of electrical tape is still on the window, but the wooden objects with the uneven geometries are missing from the mantelpiece. Only this is not a dream, she is living.

She walks on the very quiet street thinking none of the leaves that are hanging from the trees were attached to the trees when the person who is now dead was living. They are not coincident, the dead or the leaves.

Although this quiet street has a coincident relation to herself.

She wishes to buy an encampment, but all the things that are for sale are less soft, more solid.

If one ghosts the houses of the dead and then moves in the same way through her own landscape, she too becomes a displacement in the pattern of things.

The pattern appearing perhaps only as a glass of water appearing on the table.

The trees mocking a shape in the sky.

Or a bird, perhaps a cuckoo, mimicking another bird in a forest. This occurs only once and so one cannot be disturbed by it, a disturbance requiring a pattern or a repetition that cuts through a pattern or a repetition occurring outside of itself.

On a map she notices a dense forest, filled with rabbits cocking their ears as they chew grass as if listening, but they cannot really listen as this is only a sheet of paper and so no sound is emitted from its surface.

Even in the fading dusk light the metal geometries being dismantled from a construction site hold onto the blue in them, hold onto the red in them, a kind of tincture of color in them even more intense than what one may expect of the midday sun.

On the wall a painting of gulls in the sky.

Purple light appears above it then, but she cannot articulate the sky and the light into one solid shape.

She sees a person in a soft red plaid shirt in a red velvet room so vividly she thinks that the person must still be sitting in a soft red plaid shirt in the same red velvet room, only that is not true.

They have gone elsewhere, perhaps merging with the surface of the sea.

Or she sees a red-haired girl in her bed. She is there too, although she is standing to the side watching, still dressed. She feels she has seen something that should not be seen, something hidden at the heart of the world or underwater. She thinks that she will always remember the girl, her redness. But when she sees her again a few years later, she does not recognize her. Or she is not the same girl, the two girls having separated in the movement of time, so that the first girl does not exist even though she has left a red trace of the world inside of her, the other girl in this scene.

She walks along the streets lined in red brick.

As they enter winter, the green bodies of the parrots move closer to each other in their giant collective nest.

She sits among the plants in the window.

The world approaches this as a space without causation.

She sees someone being photographed.

Their entire shape is contained in one plastic bag, stretching it, or several drops of hot pink wax have fallen on the white tiles of the bathroom.

She describes a haze followed by intervals of pain.

But what is packed inside cannot be described entirely as a surface.

Or the tent appears suddenly within another container.

She sees everything too precisely, the pink steel wool covered in pieces of aluminum foil, each of the colorful round balls sitting in a candy dispenser, a miniature landscape with a lake, a dog with a purple leash poised to descend down a set of stairs, pink gum that someone has used to draw on a tree trunk, white berries on a bush that pop when they are stepped on.

She thinks about how the term optics is being used to indicate a co-presence of things that may not be causally related.

△   △
　△   △

As she moves, she leaves the tracings of her movements in the everyday of things.

You step on an acorn and the sea closes, something orange in it, the color of a cantaloupe but less yellow, recedes in it.

This is a closed shape as a dome of a forest hut or a cave may be.

This closed shape, a closed form, orange but brighter and more faded, is a kind of body hovering for an instant over another body curled in its clothes on the made surface of the bed.

It is early morning and the body of the German Shepard has not appeared yet between the trees, under a blue rope, in the woods.

A baseball lands on someone from the sky and is almost caught.

The present wind contains a distance inside of it.

She feels a sideways thing moving in a pattern as if a body were to announce another direction, take the sound being made elsewhere into an elaboration that retains a residue of the previous shape.

As a scent reoccurring brings the feeling of grapes sitting on the table, the coconut bread, the half open door, although none of these items are visible here or can be held.

The surface of a room opens to one wide shining rectangle full of the infinite movement of the trees and the lit downward slopes of streets and the air that has arrived through the medium of the forest, the running water, the separating fur of rabbits.

She wants to create a shape so wide or stretched across that it can contain anything. In a tiny grid, in its left corner, some increments of detail like dust or small red insects found underneath rocks, the rice or beans used to make an outline of a fish on a piece of paper.

△   △
 △   △

Two figures carry a cake under a cloudy plastic dome. The cake itself is white and plain but on the surface, in the center, there are small scattered shapes in different colors made out of wax or hardened sugar.

She thinks about how a city that she first visits never forms around her again when she appears in the same city for the second time. That first city lost somewhere by the docks.

Or how the feeling disperses from things and so no narrative forms or even the more translucent gradient of what could be called mood.

There is no mood, only the discernment of objects, the gravel and sand left in heaps, the movement of the river, the wooden posts left after the docks were removed, the mallards moving in the water. These can all be sensed but they do not enter or compose a story.

"What if no story appears again," she asks.

Two men are painting a fence black, but the cloth they have placed on the ground underneath the fence to shield it is made of seventeen different colors: the blues and yellows and greens in discernible edges of protective lines around other invisible objects.

She wants to be directly in the movement of the wind, in the movement of the trees, on a green street.

She wants something to appear, to open, to become discernible.

The contained rounds of the cactus are covered in hundreds of yellow needles, clustered into tiny islands. She sees each of the objects positioned in a window of waiting.

They form shapes but the shapes are also thoughts.

She annotates the surfaces of things that appear in the cloud notebook: a) the blue scrawl of dripped paint on the sidewalk b) the shimmer of the red or gold plush pants sailing c) the black strip of encased leaves formed into half circles on the molding d) the scrunched up plastic bag someone is holding in their hands e) the blue broom left leaning against the fence next to the woman bent over in a white dress touching plants.

An acorn falls on her head as the wind picks up in the trees.

This is an event.

A man standing in a light pink silk shirt for instance, his body almost visible through the sheen of fabric.

Or the man who dives inside of a tiny sphere deep beneath the ocean and communicates with a person on the surface via radio, describing everything that is visible to him but not to her. The woman in this scene.

She considers the problem of style, and style's shadow within these instances.

Something is removed as though with a dry eraser or a sponge.

The sponge is dripping water onto the stairs.

Someone makes her stand in the corner sharpening a white eyeliner pencil, which keeps on crumbling into creamy bits.

This is her socialist childhood.

△   △
△   △

Language, like movement, is the medium of the everyday and so someone moving in precise shapes leaves animate tracings in the forms of things.

She is within the slanted movement of the storm, its long division—a sheet divisible into fine white parts and divisible again into dust, all occurrences of dust in a poem.

She is here, in this hotel, inside the fine dust of the storm, and this other is still coincident, still alive, and yet unmet somewhere in the storm's surface.

On the wall two portraits of pheasants in green frames, a suggestion of light, its bright cold whiteness formulating a corner.

The interiors of wet streets or the wet leaves and what is held enclosed, pulled away beyond them in the interiors of things.

She falls out of narrative or peers at the enclosure within which narrative occurs, pressing her face against the lit wall of the building's interior, its comings and goings.

She wants to say, "this is the night, its minimal mood."

One can begin a story from something anterior to the story, a passage like an alleyway left between buildings as a form of history, or the wooden casings of things, the paneling of the room's surfaces, not quite moveable edges.

Above each lit thing a circle of ossified plants in plaster or how he positions them, the stilled lizards and fish within the suffocating mold, until they are away from air, removed from its knowledge and so stilled again, retaining all impressions of scales, the tiny imprints of the aerating pores of skin now rendered solid.

Rubber presses sound against the wet surface of the street,

leaves each lit enclosure an invisible, unrevealed world.

She wants to make a pattern that can contain anything.

The wet snout of the night fox touching the glass surfaces of its dark enclosure, outside the midday sun striking the surfaces of objects with warmth.

The surface of the pebbles on which we arrive like on another planet, covering our faces.

"This is the surface of another planet," he says.

A black dog runs in her dream through many hallways, as she is trying to suture this unmet dog with the one that had been living, its body running into the cool surface of the lake, its mouth picking up a stick and dropping it, its last day.

Or where another body's skin meets its seamless folding-in without parts.

This indivisible thing, its smell or orientation in the air like the wide leaves pressing the window's interior.

She thinks of the repetition of her walk to the trees, looking at the window from which she used to look out at them, now exterior to herself.

She writes in her cloud notebook: "The edge of one's time is unknown."

Someone arrives with oranges in a paper bag.

She sees a woman covered in black lace lying on the bed's surface, in a language without events.

Nothing happens here.

Or if she were to tell it, she would not record a story.

△ △
△ △

In the cascading maroon fur pasted in increments or tufts: a pale yellow house.

She sees a green pile of moss there positioned like a sea urchin.

She writes in her cloud notebook: "When taking the sea urchin spines out of your foot, find unripe figs on a tree and pour the milk out of their green stems."

There, in the desert, the body occupies the interior of another body, its skin sensing in two directions, further toward the interior and also toward another skin wrapping it.

The wall pulls the color of the mountain into itself, the mountain not always being that color of sour cherries, a liver or another organ, the tissues withheld from vision, from being within air.

She writes in her cloud notebook: "A caterpillar casts one skin off while another skin beneath it touches the interior surface of the skin being cast off."

The sky opens.

In the night while running to the car she is frightened by the skull of a cow resting on the table. It is raining. A powerful cat sits in the woodpile, the landscape blue beneath the branches. She has gone, or is going there, the way they would say of breath.

These two surfaces carry distinct voices, then nearly a forest.

"A lake is an article followed by a noun," she thinks.

Someone else had fallen asleep in the wet landscape. The blue appearing almost invisibly above the red branches. At the exits of colors other colors appear. Or when something is removed, a brightness enters another shape.

A figure appears to be moving in a felt line, but when seen from the sky the shape of the occurrence is unforeseen.

In the winters of herself.

She thinks about what a voice may be and its quiet, the quiet that sits behind things as blue paint.

The eyes move through the winter of post-industrial towns, their gowns having been removed, a row of angular, white, inset chandeliers standing nowhere.

This landscape places her outside of how she might have anticipated knowledge.

A curtain is something moving down a tree, being almost the same color as the tree, so that the occasion of its movement is nearly not seen.

In one hand increments like broken white stones.

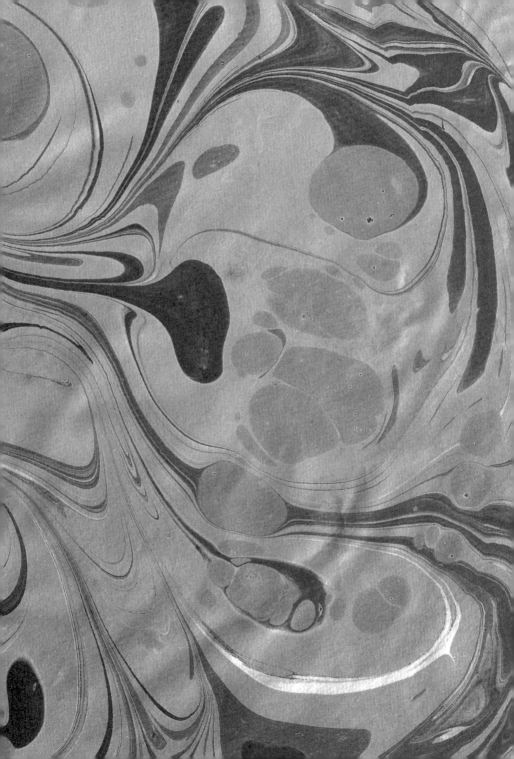

the sensation 'blue' becomes the 'blueness'
of the sky, the sensation 'green' becomes the
'greenness' of the lawn, and so forth / we
recognize the sky by the feature 'blue' and
the lawn by the feature 'green'
or the blue of the plums
is the memory of the sea
or she is wrapped in cloth with roses on it
with roses on it
or it is snowing and the men leave
or it is snowing and she cannot see
to preserve a fruit is to contain
another time of sunlight in it,
like playing charades with the faces
of those who have disappeared
to see what one cannot see

The notion of the sky as a kind of memorial or duration.

Descriptions of tents and encampments / those kinds of images of cast cloth.

Image of people waiting in line for bread or water. Image of people cutting trees in a city park for firewood. Image of people being evacuated on an airplane or a bus. An image by subtraction.

"She allows others. In place of her. Admits others to make full. Make swarm."

—Theresa Hak Kyung Cha

The trees enter where the walls had been / narrative reoccurs in each cut.

Emotions are the only way of having the world repeat itself.

A history of liquids.

The multiple sea dreams. Two.

The lining of the world is supple soft. A snail has secreted a thin sheath of slime around itself. This is written on a blue piece of paper.

"various materials and objects, including a metal bowl, yeast, flour, water, and a mirror"

An apparatus is a fragmentation of a brittle star's arm.

nacreous blue deposits of mussel shells / elaters with helical bands of blue and green flicking with changing moisture

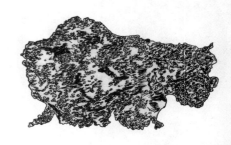

unfold like a green lollipop full of slanting white lions behind a bush made sick in twilight / a mood is a body's precipice, like little crystals in a dish

A lab notebook or a vitrine.

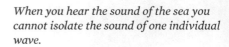

When you hear the sound of the sea you cannot isolate the sound of one individual wave.

One cannot separate a sound of one discrete wave from the overall murmur of the sea.

One individual wave cannot be heard within the overall sound of the sea.

Each perception is composed of a thousand tiny perceptions, which never reach the threshold of consciousness.

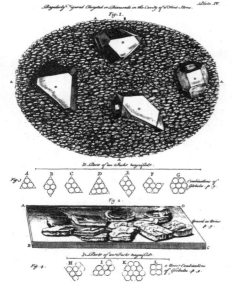

A whole world can arise out of the random movement of atoms as they bump into one another and come to make shapes, the shapes of which then come apart also; the same way an entire world can emerge out of the recombination of the letters of the alphabet as they touch one another.

Windowing an egg: In this tiny performance rub the surface of the egg like a dusty moon with gauze soaked in ethanol. Then place a piece of clear tape over an area of the egg and cut a window into the tape with a pair of scissors. A small window is cut into its shell and a piece of clear tape placed over it. Seeing the strange red moving dot. Like a tiny insect from the rocks moving along your arm.

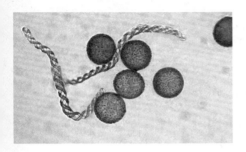

One could close the world into an orb. Shutting an appearance into things. Like a flock of blue birds rising into the mountains. A dotted seal rising from the waters. They had cracked out of the egg or had come into it. Sucking the juice out of the long threads of the thistle. A bird with blue wings turned sideways. Or a dress she is wearing made out of night.

The dark green of a cedar branch we hid beneath. She sits among the starfish. They are in different directions. A dress of yellow lemons or a fainter lemon quality, a dusk.

the sky

Some form of flight vanishes us.

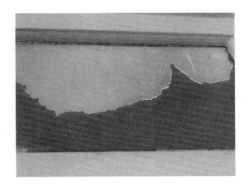

In the place where she wrapped birch bark around her wrists like an open costume. Or the temporary monument of spreading flour under her window.

"Garments worn by invisible bodies...
or petals and leaves dissolving into
formlessness."

What is tied up or clipped in loops like
a sail of an invisible boat of pink satin,
which shimmers bruised like a cherry fallen
between the embroidery of a butterfly on
the kanotjerica or the oily dark fish with
faint blue stripes pulled out of the sea's
surface. Each pass at description like a
drawing attaching at the golden loops and
dots, noticing the marks of the sea on the
fish as another kind of bruising.

she passes one piece of thread into her other
hand / or they pass them in the car not
across the border but to an adjacent point
where they exit and walk / at the other side
another man picks them up / he had driven
through the night and they drive through
the snow to the other side now / or it was
December 1992 and they were carried as
one thread reaching an edge / a thread
passing from one hand and into another

The girl eating sugar out of a paper bag.

Je tu il elle

For more than a month, eating only
powdered sugar, a woman paints her room
twice, removes the furniture, writes and
rewrites a letter to her lover, clarifying all
she had said. She spreads the pages on the
floor. She lies down and waits. Finally, her
sugar eaten, she is hungry and leaves.

how is an edge like a border

A small white room
on the ground floor
as narrow as a corridor
where I motionless
with heightened senses
lie on my mattress

The first day I paint the furnishings blue.
The second day I paint them green.
The third day I put them out in the hall.
On the fourth day I lie down
on the mattress.
And on the fifth day I move the mattress.

Instead, he disassembles the bomb and scatters its pieces. Rain begins to fall into the room through its ruined ceiling.

She has beautiful laughter as we eat the cookie dough. The bear as it lowers its body into the water of a lake has round hips like a woman.

Delicate empiricism occurs when unlike things encounter one another. The forests of May are so thick. They have positioned the neon sheet of orange paper testifying to sanitation standards next to a light pink bottle of rosé.

Use the image of the geometric solid surrounded by the forest.

How difficult it is to describe something invisible like that, and yet so solid and tangible when it is present.

All cloth is rimmed in the white lace of the sea. The light spills from the street lamps onto the highway. There is no afterwards.

When the plum passes out of the sepia toned world.

The building makes a blue rim around its exterior, which winds into the cat's mouth pink — it lays the subjectivity there caught in small tones, a shining bell or modes of speech addressed to small things with fur.

The roof of the convent on which there is a tennis court and plastic flowers. The curve of his bike on that steep street where the horse used to leap.

How to Survive on Humanitarian Aid

In April 1994, a book of recipes was published in Zagreb. The recipes were based on using the ingredients that were distributed as humanitarian aid in Sarajevo under siege. The printing of the book was supported by the World Health Organization, UNHCR, and the UN World Food Program. The author of the cookbook, Enesa Šeremet, herself survived twenty months of the siege of Sarajevo, twenty months that she calls in the preface to the book "an imitation of life." "All of the recipes offer an imaginative mode of survival and were a part of a mode of resistance of my fellow citizens," writes Enesa Šeremet.

Cottage Cheese Made Out of Rice

2 ½ cups rice
2 liters water
1 ½ spoons of vinegar
1 ½ spoons of powdered milk
2 teaspoons of salt

Cook the rice at a simmer in water for two hours. When the rice cools down, add vinegar. Combine the two and leave overnight. In the morning add powdered milk and salt. Mix into one homogenous mass and let sit for another hour. Can be served as a spread or used as a pie filling.

War Fish Stew

1 can of fish
½ liter water
1 red onion
3 cloves of garlic
3 grains of pepper
1 bay leaf
1 teaspoon Vegeta
1 teaspoon tomato paste
½ cup vinegar
1 teaspoon sugar
red pepper
rosemary

Drain the canned fish but do not throw out the oil. Take the bones out of the fish, roll it in flour and fry it in oil. Take it out when crispy and use the same oil to fry the onion and the garlic. If there is no onion, skip that step and add the fish oil from the can to the oil in the pan, then add pepper, bay leaves, rosemary and Vegeta, tomato paste, red pepper, and at the end, vinegar mixed with sugar. Add water and place the piece of fish in it. Simmer for fifteen minutes. Don't mix, but at times shake the pot. If you are lucky and have a few potatoes, cut them into circles and simmer with the rest. We know that a real fish stew is made with a few kinds of fish, but even this is excellent. If you do not have potatoes, you can serve it with polenta, pasta or rice.

Stojanka Hodžić's No-Bake Chocolate War Cake

½ cup of cooking oil
½ cup milk powder
½ cup sugar
½ cup of cocoa powder
1 ¾ cups water
8 slices of sandwich bread torn into bite-sized pieces

Place cooking oil, milk powder, sugar and cocoa powder in a large saucepan and stir to combine. Add water and place mixture over medium heat, stirring constantly until blended. Gradually add bread pieces until mixture forms single piece. Spread mixture in one oval dish and let cool. Spread War Cake Icing on cooled cake and serve.

War Cake Icing

4 tablespoons milk powder
3 tablespoons flour
3 tablespoons sugar
1 tablespoon cocoa powder
1 cup water

Place milk powder, flour, sugar, cocoa powder and water in saucepan. Cook over medium heat until ingredients form frosting-like consistency. Let cool before spreading on cake.

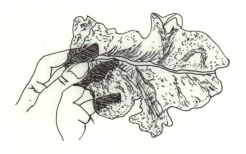

Thinking about the red rope of grief as a tiny performance.

The birds fly through the sky, passing across where the pass has already occurred.

Like the gyrations of a kaleidoscope, now rapid and now slow, its inward iridescences must be infinite, for the brain redistributions are in infinite variety.

The same flowers appear as if she had not held them. Reverse thistles or something hard and green in the middle, full of openings with feathered things. What is it that they remember as a non-shape: someone had tried to make a net / or what she keeps in the sacks suspended from the ceiling — a time manipulation / somewhere there is a full moon. In the right forepaw the cat possesses a scapho-lunar bone and an unciform bone. You want to cut tomatoes / to feel the iron scent that names the metal / like the skin of the plums dusted in blue or held in dust, as if the dust appears only where touch also wipes them away.

Now the landscape changes, the pink enters it, the seagulls come to rest on the red roof, time slows down inside the encrustations of objects.

That image of what is left on the rabbit's retina. The image of myself holding a rabbit. Combine the two.

A caterpillar casts one skin off while another skin beneath it touches the interior surface of the skin being cast off.

Resentment has a golden fertile edge that cannot be seen.

We were bank robbers and rolled in a pile of greenbacks on a motel bed.

A numb hand or face breaks into sea foam. Constellations are a thousand tiny pinpricks in the sky's sky. A gull flies over a shape of a gull in the sea. Or a gull is only the yellow edge of a window.

The red shapes disappear in the water like planets.

Through the cellophane window of a blue envelope she sees a series of points and lines drawn with a ballpoint pen. Across the ceiling the rectangles of light move with each passing car. The cut sheet has a rectangle appearing in it too, this time on a diagonal. In the distance there is a voice.

Trout Lake Park / night / a letter lost in the open.

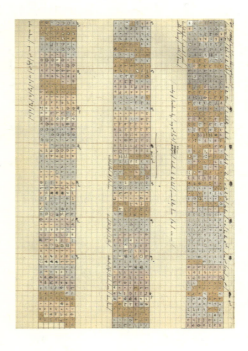

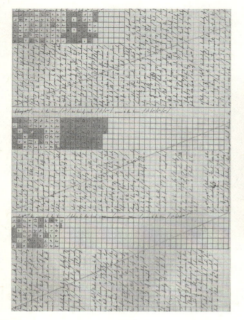

A row of black birds passes across the sky. They exit a mountain. One particular rectangle of blue brightness. They are invisible there or only make a murmuring of color, as if the blue were buzzing with the appearance of bees.

The tops of trees covered in snow like a brushed surface changing.

Arriving in Vancouver — its milk and porn stores, February 1995.

Save on Meats.

Write out of certain kinds of violence — including the violence of waiting.

Create a loose weaving as though with thick colored straw. One liquid can pass out of a tincture of another. The golden straws of nostalgia look backwards even as the movement is opening out, and yet this is what makes the moment distinct, able to proliferate through its imaginings.

a) the blue scrawl of dripped paint on the sidewalk b) the shimmer of the red or gold plush pants sailing c) the black strip of encased leaves formed into half circles on the surface of the molding d) the scrunched up plastic bag someone is holding in their hand e) the blue broom left leaning against the fence next to the woman bent over in a white dress touching plants.

1. Weave something out of thick straw of different colors. 2. During war decide between feeding the tigers at the zoo or freeing them. 3. Consider the events that are outside of human occurrences within a historical moment. Such events may be historical. 4. Consider that the door may have been made under a different regime. 5. Write a tiny performance. 6. Think about the way that one talks about a slow unfolding / the actions like the removal of things.

When mosquitoes dance in the sunset, they do not see our big human sun, setting six kilometers away, but small mosquito suns that set about half a meter away. The moon and stars are absent from the sky of the mosquito.

occurrence or a cut as an access poi.

The edge of one's time is unknown.

When taking the sea urchin spines out of your foot, find unripe figs on a tree and pour the milk out of their green stems.

A swimmer begins her swim out to the sea.

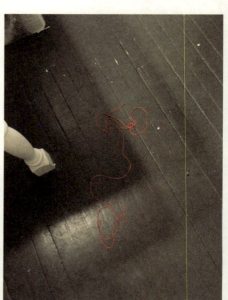

The photographs of the red rope on the floor.

tiny performance no. 1: You enter a house of the architects with twelve mice who live in the cutlery drawers. It is the first spring that you remember clearly, and so it will always stay "the spring." You walk through the gardens upwards and then climb a small wall. You think that bura (the wind) will blow you off in the opposite direction. It doesn't. Later you draw sailboats in complementary colors: orange and blue, yellow and purple, red and green. Memory is a small thing, like glow on the inside of an apartment building as you are peering in. Capitalism first appears as a proliferation of plastic objects in bright colors. You imagine the girl from London who sent you a crochet duckling in a humanitarian aid package. She imagines you. A story is a style you tell in the shape of a dream: this spring in its remembered reoccurrence, like a laurel tree in the corner of the garden, always green, crinkled and waxy. Its leaves, which you later do not recognize as what is placed/not placed in a soup.

Keeping all the objects disarticulated from their belonging: the red bowl, the disposable contact lens cases with the sheen of salt dried on them, the blue thistle flowers bought during the pandemic at Trader Joe's. In series, as a form of counting in waiting: containing time in the objects so that they can be taken out and the dream of a previous life described through them.

Everything that can be carried out of a life in a bag or a suitcase / the first calico cat running out into the hallway and then never seeing it again / not the hallway, not the red chairs, not the green edges of the windows, not the drawer with the comic books that begins to fill with the ocean / not the mouse that you may have or may not have stolen from the "mouse city," sitting in a basket on a merry-go-round, nor the mouse you find later, blind on the street, and make a nest for on the grass out of a pair of underwear.

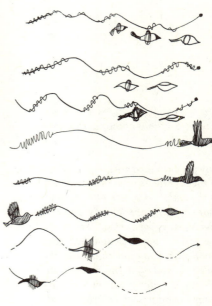

a multiplicity of tiny, fragmented regions in which nameless resemblances agglutinate things into unconnected islets; in one corner the lightest-colored skeins, in another the red ones, somewhere else those that are softest in texture, in yet another place the longest, or those that have a tinge of purple or those that have been wound up into a ball

What are the hollows or apertures of leaving?

a rust colored dress / a wall painted blue
on which water falls / it is cut out of the
sky or the sky is within it / gather all of
the elements in a hand like a blue map / a
gauze is placed on a scrape, then iodine is
poured into a corner of it, staining it red /
a bandage has a red stripe around its edges
/ she lives on a street with apples / purple
shadow on her eyes / the gesture repeats
something unknown / she cannot clean it
off / the other wall is draped in pink fabric
/ moving in a direction toward the orbit
of one place / as if you could return to the
house and the grass and have tea out of
a large cup / there are two of them / you
see one and then you see the other / if you
only knew the memories that dress brings
back to me: the sea, the mountains / some
element repeats itself in a loop in the quiet /
the scent of the lemon trees / as though the
door were to open to a form of return / you
greet me with coconut bread and grapes /
the door is left open / I enter the room to
wait / she sits at the heart of the lantern
with its turning images / they freeze in a
sequence of motion playing the ice queen
game and are then seen moving / to enter
a place in a sequence / asleep again / a
yellow curtain behind her / going to bed is
the same thing again in another place / the
unclear milky glass bottles beside them and
the candy taken on the inside

There is no one physical scale that intrinsically is the scale of texture. As your plane circles over an airport, texture is what a whole acre of trees can provide. But when you're chopping wood, a single tree may constitute shape or structure within your visual field, whereas texture pertains to the level of the cross-grained fibers of the wood in relation to the sleek bite of the axe.

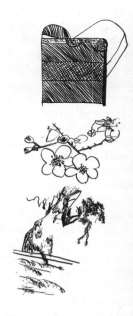

When the sky darkens, stars appear. They walk by a rose and touch it. A snake moves through the half-opened drawer of a dresser full of folded clothes. Their last conversation is about fragility, its non-existence, its assertion.

Describe the yard being cut.

This small, pink, slightly dirtied satin shoe sits in the window's interior.

A plant in a bathroom grows toward the roll of toilet paper, and as it grows, its leaves begin to touch the paper, first the big flat leaf stroking its underside like a shelf and then the little leaf making a small roof or a window above it.

Descriptions of Invisible Objects

In this tiny performance place napkins in a basket. Some of the napkins are so transparent that you unfold them into a square and press them against the sunlight.

In the snow the bat gets disoriented and hits the window.

The ways that I am trying to create these interchangeable women. And looking at other kinds of instances of such doubling.

"I am putting makeup on empty space / all patinas convening on empty space / rouge blushing on empty space / I am putting makeup on empty space / pasting eyelashes on empty space / painting the eyebrows of empty space / piling creams on empty space / painting the phenomenal world / I am hanging ornaments on empty space / gold clips, lacquer combs, plastic hairpins on empty space."

I remember that in summer time I once left by chance a cut lemon in a close room, and two months afterwards I found a putrefaction growing on the cut part, tufts of hair an inch high at least, and on the top of each hair a kind of head, like the head of a small snail, plainly beginning to imitate a plant.

A shape may release another shape beside it to act as decoy, the first shape being made out of flesh, and the other of an inky liquid dissolved in another liquid.

I see you so clearly, even though you are not seen any more.

The poem records the edge of the world within itself. The trees on the outside of the forest feel the world differently. The goldfish shimmer differently at the edges of a group.

Hans the horse could not do math but he could read the unconscious surfaces of bodies.

The world changed until it was full of bears and wolves and possums and hedgehogs and worms and eyes and cats and beetles, and those things without eyes.

tiny performance no. 2: In the performance you are living in a house on a hill. It runs near a seam of a steep street dividing you from the trees, dividing the houses from the trees. Sometimes at night you go into the yard with scissors and cut the leaves off plants to feel the edges of things like air. You look at the trees every morning and sometimes at night, placing your hands along a narrow white windowsill, so that only your forefinger and thumb touch it, so that only the outside edge of your hand touches it, or your left hand touches it, or you hold your thumb, forefinger, and middle finger so near each other that they are touching the air of the space they are not touching, pointing to an opening. A necklace has a long silver tube in it that allows emotion to pass through it. Nothing passes, rather it moves the time around itself, which then separates like a cloth or a fold in a softer, more liquid substance.

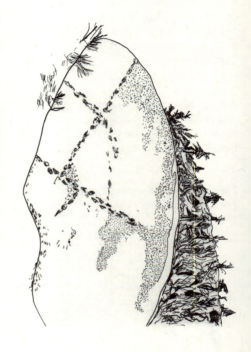

Often we are ourselves struck at the strange differences in our successive views of the same thing.

The German Shepard moves between the trees in this story. He feels guilty for looking a little too long at the other two kissing.

The common sunstar is found on rocky bottoms, coarse sand and gravel. Very small sunstars are sometimes found in rock pools.

It is reddish on top with concentric bands of white, pink, yellow, or dark red. It is white on the underside.

They move between death, trying not to see it. In a sports game the white lines delimiting the field circumscribe the occurrence of risk, its measurement.

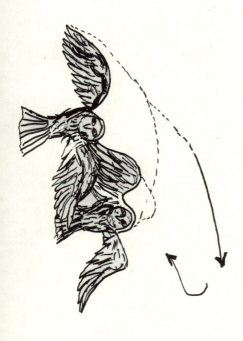

The noise of the sea is made up of an accretion of individual waves, each imperceptible, except in their summation. Within each conscious perception there is a sea of tiny perceptions, too small to be distinct, except as an atmosphere or a mood.

She throws a rock wrapped in cloth across a field of grass and shallow streams of the zone. This movement, this divination, is about finding something in the future, where the future, the field, is indistinctly also the inside, also the mind.

Slowing the rate of perception as a form of delicate empiricism.

The red threads I have put in my hair.

A museum for the poem.

A23

What is the role of the visible and invisible here?

"Each portion of matter may be conceived as a garden full of plants, and as a pond full of fish. But each branch of a plant, each limb of an animal, each drop of its humours, is also such a garden or such a pond. And although the earth and the air interspersed between the plants in the garden, or the water interspersed between the fish in the pond, are not themselves plants or fish, yet they still contain them, though more often than not of a subtlety imperceptible to us."

tiny performance no. 3: How to ask a question in such a way that it gives someone as many chances to be interesting as possible? "She takes each of her 22 sheep a bowl with its breakfast," for instance. But "there are not 22 but 23 bowls, that is, always one too many." Or you are folding pieces of paper into three-dimensional shapes. There are pyramids and cones, cubes and solids of all shapes, irregular and regular geometries. Sometimes the paper is white or yellow, sometimes it is tinted pink or touched with gold. In front of you is a small table, the shape of a small flat sea. Each shape is wrong in some way. You set them out on the table, one by one, as they are made. Inside of the inaccuracies of each, something appears: a shimmer or a tint, not pattern or form but movement on the way to somewhere.

tiny performance no. 4: In this tiny performance you are writing a book on softness. The trees move every day, not like the wood in Macbeth, which moves in premonition before an event occurs, but with a difference inside them dividing time into a finer, more granular time, a time of a bat or an insect. They are always moving, even when there is no wind. Although to say that something is always moving is to cut into it.

Now the landscape changes, the pink enters it, the seagulls come to rest on the red roof, time slows down inside the encrustations of objects.

She enters a swimming pool. A fortress looms large above it in changing light. Birds gather around a green fountain. No one is kissing.

Time is a material. The dancers move in a white room in and through the blue light. She hears laughter in the trees.

Underneath the laughter someone loses a letter. This occurs several years later, or it occurs previously.

The ethics of the dust: mineralogy as subject formation.

Detalj iz kataloga Izložbe ručnih radova bosanskohercegovačkih izbjeglica u Galeriji Kulturnog centra bosne i Hercegovine u Zagrebu

The long lines of the wing feathers fall downwards. At the red crest of the face, the purple rays of sea bone. The yellow behind it, and the thread and what is vertical and what lies flat. She is pulled into the depths by the tangle of ropes and a piano, her skirts lifting. Seeing the small holes in the black stockings. Sea urchins lie there too and the blue that is inside a wing.

The brittle leg of a starfish, the cloth latched like a sail or in the shape of a ship, the gold thread hanging from it.

What is tied up or clipped in loops like a sail of an invisible boat of pink satin, which shimmers bruised like a cherry fallen between a chest and a tree. The embroidery of the butterfly on the *kanotjerica* or the oily dark fish with faint blue stripes pulled out of the sea's surface. Each pass at description like a drawing attaching at the golden loops and dots, the flickers of thought. As if exhaustive and separate at once, noticing the marks of the sea on the fish as another kind of bruising, where the flowers left on the glaze of the biscuit are nearly inedible, some like twisted gold ribbon or gold leaf, a kind of rose we cannot touch.

*"in our relationship
i am the object/you are the subject*

*in our relationship
you are the object/i am the subject*

*in our relationship
you are the subject/i am the object*

*in our relationship
i am the subject/you are the object"*

The clouds are a flicker of a moon tent, a kind of memorial that can be sent up as figures carved out of the snow and given names and left to melt.

tiny performance no. 5: You are stitching envelopes out of large sheets of paper on a bus with red thread, with red thread. The sheets covered with drawings of the stars-as-dots by Vija Celmins. Your arm stretches in the space of the air above and to the side of the seat in front of you, against the white dots, against its blue upholstery. The red thread makes a scraping sound as it passes through the paper. The red thread comes from the materials of the House Of Dust: the brick you removed from your house, pulling one out without anything else moving, and the gravel you stole from a constructions site at night, carrying it all in a suitcase on the bus to the city where the performance happens.

"My work, until now, in one sense has been a series of metaphors for the return, going back to a lost time and space, always in the imaginary. The content of my work has been the realization of the imprint, the inscription etched from the experience of leaving."

"Here where the black moon shines; there, where the white pathway fades into the night; between reverie and resistance lies a familiar face: that of the Absent — the artist-poet who assumes the ancient role both of a medium and of a magnetizer."

"To her falls the magical task of resurrecting voices and looks by letting shadows appear and speak in her folds."

On the sheets of time.

Carried from the car, you could only be a small body / the time folding inside of you like a bone / the cat has multiplied in your dreams, become more than one identical cat you have forgotten somewhere / how the birds still fly where the trees had stood in their sparseness / now the figure seems clothed and not simply stone as if they had dressed her / someone has blinded the house, has hung paintings in the shell of ghosts.

the blue cloth over the purple cloth / the yellow stretched the rope passed through it and stretched from the center / a kind of purple enclosure like a tulip or something sharper with teeth pointing at the flat sky / the gold replacing the statue within the folds of cloth / or a ghost made of plastic bags / as if shimmering clouds / or the gold ropes hang from it / glassine and cellophane / this 17th street ghost

The plastic shapes of the tents with the blue capital letters UNHCR inscribed along their sides and the smaller gathered cloth, black squares on blue cloth, or red stripes among purple stripes over sticks, so that one may be uncertain whether there is a space to crawl into here, if this is entirely an outside without an inside.

Or in the first snow speckling the hillside an almost greenish shape with red lettering or stain on the front / so much depends on a basin overturned on its side or the clothesline where a red striped shirt hangs beside the others.

Or a carpet placed on the side like a door and pushed back to create a fold or an inwardness of cloth, like a lake formed from a black coat, which she stretches to form an island and the water, an underneath to an arrival.

The metal wires hold a small gray tarp thrown over the second draped surface, more of a peak than a roof, their skirts are blue and neatly folded underneath the knees where the yellow cloth falls on them. This is not quite the inside with further slits and recesses visible.

In the lit room with the orange tablecloth rimmed in shells or embroidery finding rest on the green mats on the floor. What is it to open a door of a house, an image in the mind that is found in the order of objects.

She enters her van to smell an apple and unfold a paper "glass" within which a piece of chewed gum is folded inwards as if held in cellophane, like a smile. These are the residues of a world, each an unfolding as in the space of a stem, the impossibly small can be hidden even before it enters.

the blue of the screen blank
indirectness and then a red rusty velvet
angel dust / the flowers growing behind the tent
the static in her dress or the shadows of leaves
a fountain spraying water
writing as a form of distraction,
somehow having caught the rim where the sun
hits the shadow or its moving line
light lilac glasses and sandals scraping a shape
in sand / the summer leaves on the trees
as a containment of time
a cat runs across a bench
a blue scarf or bag streams after her
the orange flowers with the ribbed leaves
the gesture of applying lipstick
the mouth narrowing / or her hiding behind
a blue handkerchief with flowers
the sunlight on her leg / a long path in shadow
next to a stone wall / following
one following another
pulling a finger through a curtain
writing next to objects
writing by glancing off objects
not being femme enough
the slight purple scarf around her face
the rust felt or crayon
making prints with one's hand
the mustard cover of a book
out of which she rips a page
a book called the Other Europe
a flower pinned to the edge of a dress
looking like a doll / the pigeons fly up
the stairs underneath the trees
thinking of the dense chestnut trees of May
a pink slip placed in an envelope
an azure blue robe / I am waiting
a scraped knee and a goldfish in a bowl
a goldfish that is not gold
how a smell extracts a quality
strawberries crushed in milk
a blue half planet on a piece of paper
she has a pink swimming pool
a blue balloon turns into two birds / pink and
heart-shaped / the candy that was in my mouth
carrying the flowers with the long stems

an orange cloth behind them
a round chalk shape
with three rectangular lines
falling out of and into a world
falling into a world
these iterative versions of a self
looking at myself across the water
if you only knew the memories
this dress brings back to me
the sea / the crushed rust velvet
little piles of cloth on the floor
a hidden chocolate held in a hand
I lost the key to the red

"To have been shipped is to have been
moved by others, with others. It is to feel at
home with the homeless, at ease with the
fugitive, at peace with the pursued, at rest
with the ones who consent not to be one."

waiting as a form of the political

tents / that inside and outside of enclosure
in the snow / a girl has found a spoon with
which to eat honey and is waiting

tiny performance no. 6: Place a suitcase
shut and flat on a chair. Use as a desk.

The artist who makes objects by putting
living things, such as lizards, into plaster.

What is the ground, oh what is the ground
of inscription or the continent of its
contents, a dispersion that will come as
white flakes in the air.

In the nocturama the white desert fox
moves from one glass wall to another.

The sense that citrus is brought to the
house of death.

A body is either in motion or at rest.

Each body moves now more slowly, now more quickly.

This is not absolute. It is simply a proportion.

It wants to persist.

When a body encounters another body, it may be undone, diminished, or enhanced.

When I eat an apple, it disappears.

Or its thoughts enter the movements in the lineaments of my tissues, in the wet spaces.

tiny performance no. 7: In the dream of the sea an elevator carries you up the mountain — almost carved into rock. Small, outstretched trees and shrubs surround the entrance in green as if smeared with a sponge. When you exit the elevator, on the other side of the mountain is the sea, which had up to that point been invisible. There is a slow street of a seaside town in early summer. When you reach the sea, you enter murky gray water and within it are visible many alizarin red starfish.

Or the encounter proliferates possibilities for touch and being touched. This may look like a burst of leaves on a stem, or the hyperbolic geometry of coral.

In dye chemistry the term lake denotes poorly soluble or insoluble salt of a water-soluble dye.

Mummified animals might have been created in order to serve as a kind of long-term prayer to carry over into the afterlife.

At one time these blackberry bushes held our thoughts in their hands, in their thorns rather, seeing as though blackberry bushes have no such parts as hands and possess the other instead.

One figure climbed down into the ravine to pick the berries, the other stood on the path reading *The Maximus Poems* out loud. The first wore a cowboy shirt with red and silver embroidery on the lapels and carried a yogurt cup to place the blackberries into. The second waited. The sounds of the moving river came up from the bottom of the ravine.

Now the landscape changes, the pink enters it, the seagulls come to rest on the red roof, time slows down inside the encrustations of objects.

A woman, a librarian, meets a bear as she archives. She washes the bear's fur in the water to undust its surface. Tiny snowflakes fall on the other side of a window, but there is no narrative, no mood. An orange peel rests in a glass.

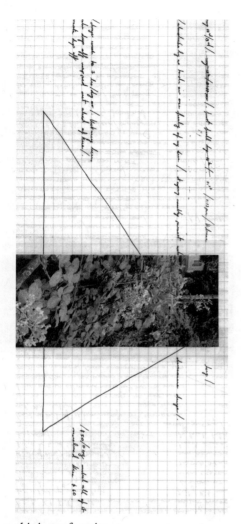

tiny performance no 8: She says: Create a forest without mentioning any of the things that make a forest. You feel it all without naming any of its names.

this is a soft entity
it has form but also a shifting edge
uncontained space
like a dream
death as being contained
in an uncontained space
that line on the pink painting
the arc in a blue room
windows of time as frames of occurrence
within which one can watch change happen

a gold color on a black
awning / birds
a ship without a mast
or the masts made everywhere
or what is familiar is in a
little circular shape
a poem does not have a place
its place is lost everywhere

There is an offset relation between this layer of time and another. The writing happens twice. Or the present can change what comes before it. The object inside is behind the object that remains in the forest, or their change is indiscriminate, not coinciding.

The snow covered the land in islands of white, we were surrounded by the water.

How looking at a figure of oneself across the water, she cannot see on the inside.

"You are the last
Who will know him
Nurse.

Not know him,
He is an old man,
A patient,
How could one know him?

You are the last
Who will see him
Or touch him,
Nurse."

That question of how one generates the feeling of numbness by creating cuts in time.

They make the pink sand into piles, the underneath texture of a fruit loop.

The textures of objects may hide the means of their production.

The bourgeoisie cheerfully takes the impression of a host of objects. For slippers and pocket watches, thermometers and egg cups, cutlery and umbrellas it tries to get covers and cases. It prefers velvet and plush covers which preserve the impression of every touch.

The worms were in love with the nuggets of gold and so they forgot about the continuities of the dirt and the inner cavities of their bodies. The worms said "lick, lick, click, click" and the gold said "click, click, lick, click."

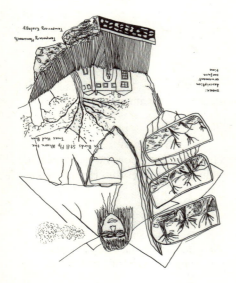

All interior space is the outside folded in / a series of invaginations that tunnel through a ball / to create spaces where things can be kept separate / small tissues some of thin pink fabric floating in the wind / the ants had come for the honey and then one night they changed their route.

The gold nuggets fell out of the cavities and landed in the dirt. The dirt was continuous like one long sheet. Sometimes it found forms of difference or separation in the long stomachs of worms. Anything contains an outside inside of it. A doughnut is a simple shape with a hole. They had entered the interior of the office building, moving through the dim corridor toward the red light.

these were formed in her imagination from a rabbit she was fond of that slept on the bed at night

as such early impressions as from a dream or plain sight of household pets can imprint themselves on what appears and should be avoided

others say that if it be a fact, a veil should be drawn over it

having become pregnant, but following her fascination with a sighting of a rabbit

of a creature resembling a rabbit but whose heart and lungs grew without [outside] its body

about fourteen days since she was delivered by the same person, of a perfect rabbit

the woman had made oath, that two months ago, being working in a field with other women, they put up a rabbit, who running from them, they pursued it

from that time she hath not been able to avoid thinking of rabbits

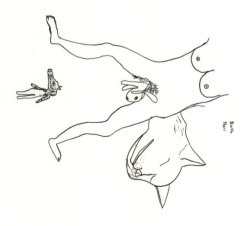

When we first heard the sound in the morning, it sounded like a tea kettle or a coffee maker. We thought that the other one of us had woken up early to make coffee. Later we saw that the sound was coming from a breathing whale that we could see through the window. The window looked like a postcard but later we saw that the tiny waves were moving in it, so we thought it was a television.

What constitutes the edge of a body if all of the body can see. In this tiny performance you are on the beach at night gathering specimens. The sea has withdrawn. The sea has withdrawn to describe the world. The edge of the poem.

Each object's position is a narrative.

We don't know what a body can do.

It's not liquid, it's not substantial.

The bowl of it like a translucency in the paper on which two faces can be seen in what seems to be an inlet of dusk, or is it sky, as to account for lightness and for shape in the room in which you paint the wall blue, as if to shift something in the occlusion. And later she paints an arc of white over it, a pool of plexiglass lit from underneath. The sky has disappeared, but it is not entirely dark yet and the birds are still singing, are in the air. What are these instants of time, getting off the bus to buy some porcelain into which two pink figures step, and the understanding of the inside of it so dry like a voice in whisper, a kind of plaster one cannot see in the forest even though the forest is deep and dark like a story. It is there in the stepping, the lightness of it, a late spring day, its translucency in the blue not like an egg. The grayness of the sky and their distant flight in the cold wet air, summer but not summer and the sea too cold. Is it always that they are in flight, too fast in movement to be seen as moving at all, like a stick placed in front of a snail, too fast in animation, the rhythms of the white flowers opening, opening then closing.

a sound of hair being cut
the dream is of cloth or what she sees: oranges
and blue flowers on cloth
the world is cut through
we cannot see its inside
the blue of the plums is the memory of the sea
how is the material of the present
the dust on the plums
a memory of another world before
the blue of Adriatic turning
into the green of Pacific
the storm finds them out of nothing:
carries them in the blue cave
she throws fabric over water
for them to walk on
we don't see anything in the snow
stretched with blue silk like the ocean
between the fingers
a naming of the islands in the
Adriatic Sea:
Korčula, Mljet, Hvar, Pag,
Krk, Cres, Lastovo
we count them and I tell you about
uncountable experience:
the water dripping between
the fingers / such glancing things
as if the body deflected them
in noticing the winter light
you shake the cat to awaken it from deep sleep
to reassure yourself away from death
reading its gums
the small sedimentations
of glistening white teeth
so unlike yours

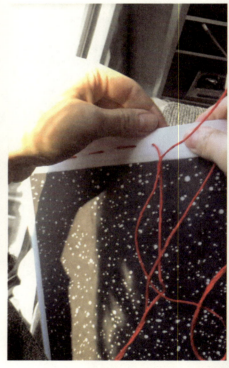

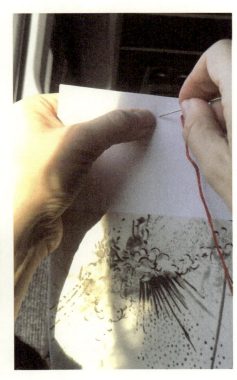
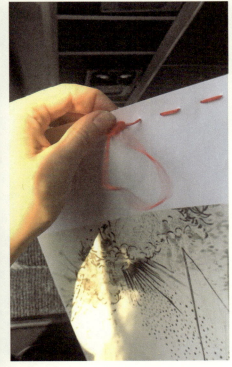

The boys are gemlike.

Mosquito Astronomy

When mosquitoes dance in the sunset,
They do not see our big human sun,
Setting six kilometers away.
They see small mosquito suns
That set half a meter away.

The moon and the stars
Are absent from the sky of the mosquito.
The moon and the stars
Are absent from the sky of the mosquito.

Mosquito astronomy. Mosquito
astronomy. Mosquito astronomy.
Mosquito astronomy.

A mosquito buzzing and fluttering
Under the dome of a 'mosquito sky,'
Seeing through its tiny compound eyes
Many tiny proximate suns.

No moon and no stars.
Just many warm orange globes.
As close as an orange on the table.
As close as an orange in your hand.

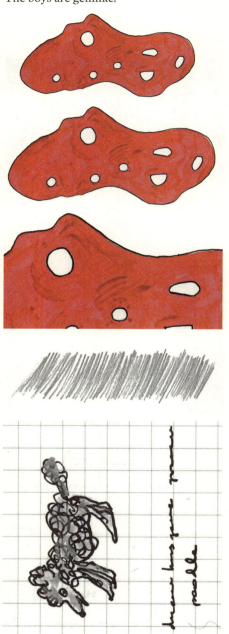

*The first generation of asymmetry:
a pink map of rock galaxies, the earth
turned upward and spread as faint pink
left in the cornices of things, the blush of
stones as the forgotten discs of dreams.
Such is the succulent self — one with the
interior eyes. The impossibly thin matter of
the flasks. Sucrose is one struck by the held
translucency of the object. What does it
mean to have been laid to rest on a jeweled
surface, what one may turn around into
the shape of the sky.*

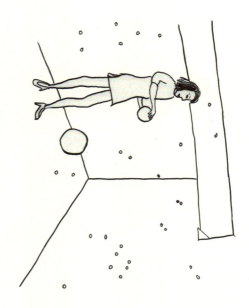

The body is a problem, its disappearance,
its inlaid horizon. A discernment is also
an orifice. Their legs crossing in the blue
porcelain of what luck has gathered.
The body is not objective because it is
elsewhere and cannot imagine itself in
space. A distribution in a room, of dust, of
small flies, a citron color oozing between
fingers. The blue parakeet freezing during
the war.

"Gold was used to cover the eyes and
mouth of the deceased, probably with the
intent of preserving their ability to see and
speak in the afterlife."

Is the cloud notebook a space of perception?

The *pealed* orange as oil in a gray glass
/ a discernment of qualities. The queer
ephemerality of form. A model of time
that is not about ends...

"Only one animal, a female black bear, remains alive of the 100 there when the siege began in April. She is mangy, perhaps half her weight as when her ordeal started, and she barely has the strength to stand upright against the rusting bars of her cage when visitors arrive with a loaf of bread and a few snatches of grass."

"After surviving the siege for more than 200 days, a bear, the last surviving animal in the zoo in Sarajevo, has died. 'We took her some bread and an apple last week, but she was too weak to eat them,' Pal Takač, a zoo employee, said Tuesday."

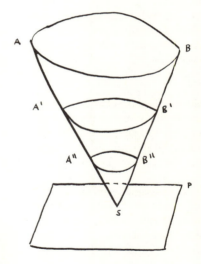

tiny performance: no. 9: In this tiny performance you are the girl in the snow. Like a sheet in time you cannot see yourself. A figure placed in the distance looks outward.

A curtain of gender descends between us.

the hands on the windowsill / the snake moving through the drawer in Black Moon / how one generates the feeling of numbness by creating cuts in time

What would this be as a film?

Thinking more about the coverings for the mouths and the eyes of the dead.

They make the pink sand into piles.

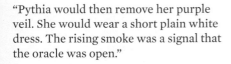

"Pythia would then remove her purple veil. She would wear a short plain white dress. The rising smoke was a signal that the oracle was open."

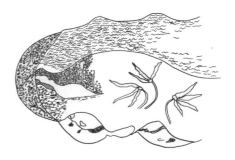

"Await not in quiet the coming of the horses, the marching feet, the armed host upon the land. Slip away. Turn your back. You will meet in battle anyway."

"You will go you will return never, in war will you perish."

"You will go you will return, never in war will you perish."

"You will go you will return never in war will you perish."

tiny performance no. 10: At the shoreline or edge of a lake or a sea, look outward to see a version of oneself that cannot see the figure looking out. Through a slit in the wall they place the food for the dead. The girl in the snow cannot see herself.

this heard in the rustlings of oak trees / or within the flight of wild pigeons at Dodona

What of a bowl holds the sky. Some in the open shape depart. The links in the yellow stamens that are the buds on the long stems that are the sea surrounded by figures, the exile finds them.

Where something is found may not tell us of its departure. The objects that cluster the present are only a crease in the firmament of occurrence. A fold in the fold.

Often we are ourselves struck at the strange differences in our successive views of the same thing.

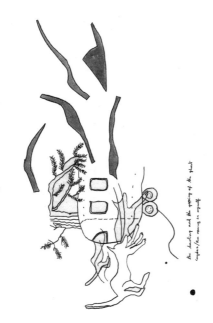

She lives in the house with oranges, white blossoms that I remember as a hidden shack with an open window, where she hides the doll by the fireplace resting on a blanket. She gives her the middle name Rose. And in the interim thinking about the white relief of the palm leaves on the wall painted over. Entering the bus stop so many years apart, like water moving in two opposite directions. At times the line of transformation is also the edge of the fingers moving beneath the trees. You sit in the beaded curtain, wearing a red dress, the plant's soul in front of a mirror in front of which you have hidden. She hangs these tissues from the ceiling, knowing that something comes from blood, from the thinness of the inner body, its many sheets of listening. The body, a series of folds of the outside space inward, a kind of entrance. A subtle body, a kind of mobile thing of invisible liquids, like a painting of a ship hung on a wall when you are waiting.

To hold an enclosure from underneath with one hand in that gesture slowed down into an existence even after it passes.

The overlap of cloth positioned on sticks, how it slightly peels or leans like an overlay, the gray on light beige, at times a flatness or a curve of a triangle.

Or the rectangles entirely shining blue like the sky.

Or she is skipping over a jump rope in the sand in between other ropes tying the shapes down into gray stretched things. Ahead is maybe the sea tied to the shadow of a rope. Yellow divided by white stripes next to a long purple shape distorted by wind.

Or a green rope stretched above a blue and white sheet, not knowing how to divide the decorations even though she had come from a mountain weaver among the rocks and little dirt in the dark wood.

Or this cloth the color of purple anemones surrounded by the waves of blue shadows stretched on a metal frame facing away in yellow shawl.

Or the uneven ground with something lilting on it at the border, blue again but this time dusty and not evenly bright in the long grass, a blue figure with a bird bent over or upright.

Or different blues, turquoise plastic sheets rough to the touch with a threaded feel of little windows, and that other blue, more extinguished, watery, the distance made up of other squares of blue, far and divisible.

Or a space divided in orange, in a blue wreath in a skirt or in a basin.

Or a red dress in which she is with blue flowers.

Or sheer netted space, the world visible through it taken from inside, a sheet with red flowers.

Or printed fabrics holding the thought of a plant, of a memory invisible through the sheer shapes lit as shadows within.

Or she is wearing pajamas with hearts on them, a blue bucket being filled with water, clearly summer. A girl in a yellow dress with dots on it, or a long purple draping shape in the sun drawing water.

A black skirt with red flowers, holding above one's head a gray imprecise sheet or blue slats of plastic on cloth, a faded red shape draped across a rope with a white rim and a series of dots.

The world made again
A red skirt billowing in observation

The door of the poem opens
A blue line or thread stretched between things
A person reading looks like another person

"The tree greens," she says.
"The bowl is cut."
"The bowl is not cut, it is upturned."
They paint the inside blue to approximate the sky.
Just like they paint the overhang above the door blue to ward off ghosts from entering the house.

The marble answer is in its rimmed shape.

Smoke cedar ice cream.

The reparative three-dimensionality of the object.

tiny performance no. 11: Open a bag of flour and turn it over so that all the flour falls onto the table or a cloth placed on the ground. Using your hands pat the flour, down until it makes a small dome shape, not unlike a soft cake. Place a piece of chocolate in the center of the flour. Each participant should have a thin, silver spoon with which to take small slices of the flour cake. Before shaving off their sliver of flour, each participant should describe a house they had once lived in. The performance ends when the piece of chocolate falls to the ground, upon which the person who dislodged it must eat the chocolate without the use of their hands.

What is countable or uncountable time
Each day the eyes close
The red head of the female woodpecker pecking the tree
seasonal the wood is opening

How a poem that has so many registers of aesthetic form as blocks of reoccurrence says something about that feeling of migration. Think of these as kinds of notes on exile.

How the poem creates an inside and also closes it.

She looks at herself from a distance of time.

Trout Lake Image

There are stairways and cracks in the fabric of summer / she is also another / the heavy new leaves of the chestnut trees / a cat runs across two benches at the edges of shadow watching the invisible / a feathered thing / red shoes and a stairway / cast out forms of shadow / she touches a wall / the cat is in red flowers / a blue bag stuffed with cloth and a blue car / a place that is left never changes / the umbrellas in the sun, each wing of them another color / a red stamp.

tiny performance no. 12: Expose a piece of black cloth to the falling snow and observe a variety of curious figures that gather on it.

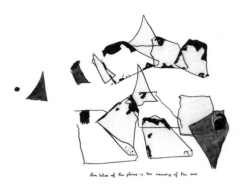

A photograph of pigeons on a wall of a room.

How a silk object draped on a chair contains a small landscape in it.

An old woman changes size.

A snake moves through a drawer.

The flowers begin to cry out as she steps on them.

She is wearing a pink cardigan.

They throw rocks wrapped in cloth to determine the future.

The open field changes in relation to their thoughts.

The inside and the outside are different from one another, but they may not always be apart.

The leaves on the tree flicker, some visible and some known but invisible in the darkness.

The body visible, spotted, underneath the pale blue curtain of water.

In the disappearing the farthest distinctions appear, a birch tree in the distance in front of the blue hills, for instance—it is not necessary to go far, as something overtakes it.

She considers the night's firmament, the clear blue light also lit.

The landscape makes of color the shortest possible day, the white stone resting between the trees in a room, its minutes passing.

She wishes that non-existence possessed a subjectivity, that it could run across a field, that something could run across a field to greet her.

A voice carries even though it is not a color, its shapes having now become distinct. Why the blue holds longer to the object's edges?

It is hard to trust the movement in the trees. The wind too is an apparition or an appearance.

She considers the night, its increments of shadow as a carrying surface.

The birch tree spreads into hundreds of branches at its tips, there between it and the sky.

She is drawn there to this one curve in the road because of the thin sounds that appear between the long needles of pine trees, the sky that becomes pink even though what renders it pink is invisible or hidden.

The oracle is in the syntax or where the syntax fails to part from itself, joining occasions.

The repetitions and differences in anyone make an uncountable time.

One is within the stones or positioned among the stones, one misaligns them.

△   △

△   △

She is not held by a story, although the yellow hanging bars and loops of the playground suggest a possibility of action, each object having arrived imminent through the occurrence of narrative, each plant planted in this garden or brought by the wind, the orange boxes enclosed within the billowing white plastic bags, the occurrence of a brush covered in blue paint.

"All detail is narrative," she thinks.

Even the white pipes stretching out of the white walls.

The smell of neroli.

The lack of love or its disappearance.

She thinks of the island's surface, only it is not an island but something attached.

The wetness attaches to the surfaces of leaves, in between their shadows.

She considers the possibility of sketching in her cloud notebook—the way that it allows for a recording of occurrence without concept.

Rain begins to fall more intensely.

Some children laugh in the grass.

She writes in her cloud notebook: "Resentment has a golden fertile edge that cannot be seen."

A small ceramic mushroom with a glittering cap sits in the yard's shadow.

They sit within the ship's cradle, held there by the wood, a tiny fire fractured through the lemon-yellow cool of the glass surface, shells as shapes thickened and obscured by the white paint.

The tracks of a small pyramid or a pile of sticks, the food left for the dead in golden dishes, or a landscape that is seen through or appears in the silk of a dress, a slit in things that permits movement between the worlds.

She writes in her cloud notebook: "We were bank robbers and rolled in a pile of greenbacks on a motel bed."

"It takes time for currency to be taken out of circulation," he says.

She leaves a small pile of berries below a tree then, there are no golden dishes, only the red reverse cones of their shapes, a knitted world of coral, the ski slopes of a body.

Then 1,500 years pass, and dust and light make further shapes on the rivulets of the glass, its already marked surface, and yet this one thing is unchanging.

It changes only as we look backwards at it, our gaze the changing thing between it and the lit glass, which permits only the anterior movements of things.

The perspective of the girl in the snow does not know the unfolding thing, the thing that is to meet her.

△   △
　△   △

The blue beetles crawl across the ground, tiny numerous drops of sky, a blue bridge, fake teeth that a woman models out of bread dough and covers with white nail lacquer, a lattice through which the river is green or a thought is green pressing into a wall.

Later she presses them into and over her real teeth, like little lacquered shells and goes out into the evening, its sky.

Later she becomes a tree with round leaves in a blank landscape, the gulls resting their faces near each other.

Everyone and no one looks at the tree, someone leaves berries underneath it, someone reaches for something inside the tree, although we can no longer see their hand once it disappears into its shell.

She writes in her cloud notebook: "A numb hand or face breaks into sea foam. Constellations are a thousand tiny pinpricks in the sky's sky. A gull flies over a shape of a gull in the sea. Or a gull is only the yellow edge of a window."

She returns to the point when all that is now yellowing had appeared at once between days, the extended things, a surface near a surface, an explosive thing, a dark green and silver recess in this thing that she calls the forest.

Everything appears between everything else that appears, she thinks. The orbits of time detach from the surfaces of the planets then.

The bright silver ping of them floating off somewhere into space, the different apples having ripened differently, the sea having warmed, and now the fuzzy sheaths appearing on the surfaces of gooseberries.

She does not remember any of this happening.

She remembers it had stayed warm for a long time.

You had walked by the fall fields, recording cattle, drinking water left in the discarded water bottles, taking pictures of signs for nail salons, confusing a dolphin with something else.

She thinks of the quiet she has come to now, her quiet, which seems as unbroken as the moving river beneath, a place a person could look at for a long time to see the things moving in it, undead.

The blue vertices of a truck almost the blue of the sea she never thinks of.

$$\underline{\triangle \quad \triangle}$$
$$\underline{\triangle \quad \triangle}$$

She tries to think of her sadness as a detailed space.

Feeling that the numbness only appears as a possibility of sensing.

A long white bench rims a rectangle of the world, between it and the sky the asymmetry that cuts a volume into two facing suns.

She writes in her cloud notebook: "A swimmer begins her swim out to the sea."

As she goes, she moves farther and farther from the surface.

She has left her cane on the beach.

In the night enclosure at the zoo a white desert fox touches the surface of the glass with her wet nose and turns around, her ears alert, hearing between things.

What if the moving patterns of the world arise out of the reoccurrence of an egg resting on a table, the appearance of blue, a wondering animal.

She writes in her cloud notebook: "Each object's position is a narrative."

A stretch of cloth parallel to the stretch of shadow and light on a ceiling.

She writes in her cloud notebook: "We don't know what a body can do."

In between the golden handles, pincers, almost like the fingers of a hand, an object sits. Perhaps it is a triangular shape cut out of stone. In the spots on the stone, blue, gray, ochre—the rectangular blocks of different fields.

She writes in her cloud notebook: "An apparatus is a fragmentation of a brittle star's arm."

She applies a color called desert rose over her lips.

She writes in her cloud notebook: "When the sky darkens, stars appear. They walk by a rose and touch it. A snake moves through the half-opened drawer of a dresser full of folded clothes. Their last conversation is about fragility, its non-existence, its assertion."

They wait to see what the tree will do, but she wishes to carry the brightness of events, to place their forms into the world, doubling it. She wishes for a contrast to the distance of the moment.

She writes in her cloud notebook: "Through the cellophane window of a blue envelope she sees a series of points and lines drawn with a ballpoint pen. Across the ceiling the rectangles of light move with each passing car. The cut sheet has a rectangle appearing in it too, this time on a diagonal. In the distance there is a voice."

She thinks of the enclosure of the world, its vertices.

She writes in her cloud notebook: "They move between death, trying not to see it. In a sports game the white lines delimiting the field circumscribe the occurrence of risk, its measurement."

Its small life has fallen into the glass and it has drowned.

In the hallway she uses her hands to make a mask over her face. For an instant it appears that a stuffed toy animal in the shape of a leopard or even a hedgehog has appeared instead of her forehead, her nose, her eyes.

One night she is invited to a party with candles. It snows outside. She has arrived, she thinks.

On a photograph of her in a blue bathing suit standing on a dock someone has written: "It must be sad to be a celebrity and know that the best way to reach your peak level of fame is to die."

The private stainless steel surfaces of a kitchen appear in a newspaper. Someone is holding a leaf to their mouth, suddenly aware that they are seen.

She finds her body somewhere on Instagram, only she is not sure that it is her body, the thighs appearing wider, different, thicker, more translucent, dusted, sunning—she cannot be sure they are her thighs.

She writes in her cloud notebook: "She enters a swimming pool. A fortress looms large above it in changing light. Birds gather around a green fountain. No one is kissing."

In the video a squirrel is hopping, a girl eats red ice cream, a parking lot appears.

In the video someone says: "I wish I had some spray to make them go away."

In the video strips of paper hang from the walls and the children are instructed to draw unicorns. One little girl wanders around yelling at the children who are drawing other animals: "You are off theme."

In the video someone cuts a slice of white cake. A man falls down the stairs and vomits a blue color. Later he is carried and then he dies.

In the video an orange song, a dance surface, a slice.

$$\underline{\triangle \quad \triangle}$$
$$\underline{\triangle \quad \triangle}$$

They sit in a red velvet room in exact positions, plaid appears as another surface between them, something divides the surface on which they are resting into two different skies.

She checks her memory of a hand against its image.

She checks her memory of a hand against the image of a hand in the video.

They are holding the same thing.

She comes into her heart then as a repetition. A gull walking on the sidewalk, or a discarded cereal box on an alpine slope covered in snow, or a milk carton resting on a green tent become the surface of the glass, the surface of the pool, the surface of loneliness, the surface of the dance floor, the surface of the sun, the surface of the yellow Ziploc bag.

Her head begins to ache.

She enters a repetition.

The slick, black fake fur of the coat moves this way or that in the wind, carried by sweat, carried by the ocean currents, carried by the weeds.

It never turns into a solid. Its surface is pink and translucent. Something pours out of it. The tiniest events occur behind the grass. And no matter how much they clean, something passes of this into the ground. A lit thing in a shape, its triangular geometry.

She listens to a fight coming from the yard in the night, plates are broken, she does not intervene, a horse circles in the snow.

She writes in her cloud notebook: "Time is a material. The

dancers move in a white room in and through the blue light. She hears laughter in the trees. Underneath the laughter someone loses a letter. This occurs several years later, or it occurs previously."

Their positions in space determine everything because of the positions in space of the other fast-moving, piercing objects. Someone counts the minutes before and after an event happens.

In the video she sees a piece of paper.

When the mulberry tree develops leaves, this is called a flush, this is called redness, this is called a window of time.

A napkin flies across the street.

An alternate alignment of the lines appears on a silver surface, someone does not return, everyone writes an apology for an event they did not conduct.

There is laughter between the trees, and a paper boat in a small lake lists, dips. This habit costs her a hundred dollars a day.

She drowns taking the risk of saving someone else from drowning. Sycamore trees are in the background.

Now, now an old man plays jazz records on the phonograph.

There is an uneven number of seats, so she sits in the middle, resting her hands on the shining copper in the half-light, its dimness. She thinks of someone else writing on the surface of her thoughts. She thinks of this as a performance that cannot, does not occur, not even in the shadows.

When she is old she will sit on the bench near the tree, knowing that this aspect of the world cannot, did not unfold, its movement having been cut so that it cannot reach us, cannot reach the beach, cannot reach the sun. And so whatever they spread in the ocean is its proximate.

In folded pieces of paper she keeps hair and liquids, on them are painted blue cubes of thought. She thinks of this as a permission, even though she does not have one.

The white tiles cover the surface of the ceiling in a perfectly silky way. She thinks of the skin of lizards she has once touched.

She becomes frightened, then unpliable, then frigid, then frozen, then brittle, then solid, then overt, then bingo, then loud, then red, then tasseled, then lopsided, then interior, then frosted, then sprinkled, then sparkled, then slow.

She writes in her cloud notebook: "The textures of objects may hide the means of their production."

She realizes that the extreme forms of exercise are not a form of loneliness.

A man puts on a bathrobe and reveals his genitals while standing next to a tree, while standing next to a desk, while standing next to a television, while standing behind a television, while standing on a hairy carpet, while pressing the front surface of his body against a window.

She feels the exhaustion of being the accountant of all such instances, of describing the visible while the invisible remains a domain unshaken by the revolutions of action.

△　△
　△　△

A poem is a surface: it shifts to contain everything, this long pink line among its waves.

A photograph taken among the waves always suggests another possible photograph.

A leaf may be ribboned, then placed in a dish, its dark shape suggesting another landscape, and so of shells when they are cut to reveal the softness between them.

To enter a new one requires a groove.

In this scene a man drinks white paint in front of a laundromat. The police are called. He sits on a bench and continues to drink white paint. Later when he is taken away, and even years later into the future, the paint continues to mark the walkway where the man had sat.

"A possible landscape also contains its impossibilities," you say.

"Some birds chirp beneath the wooden pellets left by a green wall."

In the discarded space of the canal someone has built a fountain. Or, small blue squares positioned on top of one another rim each of the windows of a building.

Their lives and deaths overlaid somehow into a vivid density.

At first she did not understand disappearance, but now it had become self-evident, a kind of hum left behind things.

Even the rose red of the bricks curled upward.

No addition was possible.

She wore a pink hat but sadness overtook her face. Small balls of Styrofoam lined the seams between buildings and the sidewalks, leaves, chirps, little black pellets.

She was somewhere that still appeared to her like a place full of unthought detail, "marble left in sheets in sunlight," not in sunlight at this moment.

Nothing lit is visible from inside of it, no flush or blush or whatever could appear in stone.

Someone tells her a story about a transparent mattress while they are waiting for a bus.

A mother leads a small girl on a leash. The girl spills some water on herself.

Everyone acknowledges that the world appears in the poem, or as the poem appears, the world appears.

A woman has tattoos of trees pressed densely on her hands so when she presses her hands together a whole forest appears.

She thinks about the mysteries of touch, someone makes a sound that is digital, someone mimes a size of a dog with their hands.

△　　△

△　　△

She finds it strange walking in the architecture after she has already seen the drawing.

She does not watch any of the videos, does not want to know any of the content.

The bronze surface greets her then. She wants to become the surface of the sea, become invisible, become divided into a thousand waves.

The light passes through a series of glasses pressed against each other. All clear surfaces lack withholding, she thinks. Laughter is a form of translucent paper, or joy.

She enters a cabinet filled with boxes of wafer cookies in different flavors, hazelnut nougat, gold rush, lemon. A woman with a voice speaks. Someone presses tiny green beans out of the green beans.

She thinks of deafness and lists and oblique angles. A red liquid rests on the bottom of the glass. Many forms of thinking are not statistical, she thinks. A city is large, chunky, unpowdered.

She thinks of albumen as a form of clarity.

Nothing is in the glass now. In the distance someone sings, a bird. A woman brings something to read between the rocks.

She has an embroidered jacket with tiny mirrors on it.

A possibility of representation opens inside of the representation. Almost any surface can act as a site of such appearance.

The bear may be any size, really.

She writes in her cloud notebook: "A woman, a librarian, meets a bear as she archives. She washes the bear's fur in the water to undust its surface. Tiny snowflakes fall on the other side of a window, but there is no narrative, no mood. An orange peel rests in a glass."

Someone next to her says, "it's too dreary. This story is too dreary and awkward."

△ △
△ △

She watches an uneven wall of bricks, which does not align with an uneven post.

She likes to read around others, to be visible, rendered to them as a participant.

Someone tells her that something can move along a surface of a geometry without ever entering the middle.

This is brave and obvious. She makes a decision about which lines to cut. She wishes for telephones, the old-fashioned ones, with cords and voices.

They repeat making the same mistake even after the mistake no longer matters: "Affirm absolutely what should only be affirmed somewhat." She wonders if this can give back anything to anyone or if this is only a prolonged delusion, a form of thinking that is fractal and infinite.

Some improvised pattern moves through her, she thinks in its sorcery, its interstices of thought. This form of being is not her own. From a tall building she watches the cars moving underneath her. She feels the unknown. Thinks of the self-created event as a puncture of time.

The discarded kernels of corn become a crispy surface. The sound that bodies make is already gone, or it is the bodies themselves that are receding as something that you see behind you in the rain.

The night swirls around a lamp or is it the lamp swirling its candy candy?

Nearby, in fluorescent police paint, the words "All Units" and a zero have been sprayed onto the hotel's driveway.

△   △
△   △

She says, "we walked through the blue building looking. The building was made out of small blue bricks, cold to the touch. Outside was the sun and inside were walls."

She says, "I pushed my hand through a mail slot and touched the other side of the wall." Outside, a truck had driven over glass bottles, spraying the sidewalk with long, wild streaks of foam.

She says, "I held a list of actions we were to do as long forms of division."

The sides of cloth across the gray cube occur at an angle,

displacing its lines in a landscape. Something within it departs from the initial surface, then something like glass or icing is crushed underfoot.

This is not a tent.

A fire catches in a camp full of horses. There is snow and fire and forms of running figures, some lit, some still hidden by the dark.

Cloth may be draped as lace over a lamp.

She listens. A yellow bird appears. It is the color of a lemon, the color of a canary, only paler. Inside of the bird is a thought, a sound it has heard, which repeats as thought. Outside, a whole field of flowers, star shaped or round, and the bees buzzing electronic.

Behind the wall the trees press against an unlit stone shape.

Small squares of prose appear, flowers in a window the color of rotting meat.

Qualities transfer between objects. A wolf runs through a field of pixels for instance, and is then not seen, not even after the event has occurred.

She considers the possibility of the event's reversal. If one were to turn an object inside out, a green sweater for instance, a forest would appear inside of it, and so a river appears at the bottom of a white cup.

△   △

　△   △

Then small forms of invisibility appear in things. She waits anonymously, wading through the golden braided ropes someone has hung from a window of speaking birds.

There is a ridge, velvet cushions the color of lips and a neon red, no a neon pink, light seen here.

"A surface has no outside if it has no inside," she says.

Or a surface may be a crack out of which something oozes, a red shining element like confetti. A dry object, whereas it had at first seemed like a wet one.

"Something shines at her then," a bright pink alarm light where a group of poodles has gathered, or a green, a green carton with dips in its surface where peaches had rested.

She feels herself folding in and in within surfaces of capitalism as within a flaky buttery croissant, her body marbled like a steak.

A long streak of water bisects a dark passage between walls, forming a latch. A lamp streams like hair.

The wallpaper made of birch trees is interrupted by the blank aspects of the wall where nothing occurs.

The rooms appear on a screen as perfect cubes, visible all at once like a centerfold.

The participants do not see the other participants.

She thinks of a dog who, having lost a sense of space before its death, is unable to stand upright and yet holds itself rigidly even while leaning. She attempts to hold the body of this dog upright in the back of the car on a highway a woman covers something with a blanket hiding it from visibility.

Someone pushes past her in a long-haired white coat. A heavy truck passes her. Someone sends her a love note about the warm exhaust of cars.

Men argue in front of a restaurant with pictures of cattle on the walls.

She meets a woman named Blue and they sit by the inflatable kiddie pool dipping their legs in the water.

Three men are sharing a story about another man and a swan in a bathroom together. Blue lights light up the sky.

This is everything that has ever occurred.

She wants a different song, one with wolves in it, one with snow in it and the trees, the frozen surface of a lake, some birds, a shrinking bear.

△   △

△   △

She considers the inside of a dumpling and whether any faces may occur there.

In a dark room someone sits drinking mint tea behind curtains. She thinks of a face, a young beautiful face lined in fur and strawberries.

She considers why objects have surfaces, little ribs and skins that are pleasurable to touch, the sensation spilling inward from them like a pink wave or a current of white ferrets running underground.

She stands by the square of the park, visible on the ground are twelve, thirteen rats where one would anticipate squirrels.

She is reminded of a mouse city she has seen once on a long table covered in little houses and Ferris wheels, cars and shops and ponds with little floating boats.

She thinks she may have stolen one of the mice then from the mouse city, having placed it in her pocket, but cannot be sure whether this actually occurred.

They cleaned the cellars and the basements, the whole underground, among the whisperings, but they did not know what would occur until those who had walked out to the streets were shot by snipers and the city was surrounded.

At times, events may occur that refigure the geometries of intentionality. It is either that the pattern of inevitability is in the mind or the world, but at times it may not be possible to tear the two apart, she thinks.

She notices a mosquito sucking the blood that is in her hand.

△   △
　△   △

Sometimes she thinks she comes from a woman with the apples, who owned a horse who knew the way from the train station to the house, or the green-eyed one, a carpet weaver, or the one who knew how to pull green beans from their hollows, and who escaped into the forest on a horse in war as a way of resisting the occupation, leaving her baby in a house with a blind room, or the one who escaped through the tunnel dug underneath the airport, or the one who spread her black coat on the ground next to the sea so that she, they, can sleep, or the one who carried the rings and sold them. Sometimes she is not sure which one she is, or if the dream of the sea, the one with the golden elevator ascending the cliff with the red coral in the blue water, the one with the red, dense flesh of anemones in the dunes, is the same dream.

△ △
 △ △

In this scene, three figures are sitting around a small pile of flour spread on a handkerchief that has been placed on the floor.

The flour is patted down into a shape of a small dome or a cake.

At each turn one of them takes a cut through the flour—this cut is as thin as a sliver.

As they cut, each speaks a sentence about a lost house.

Each sentence begins with an it:

"It had accidental fertile cherry trees growing in front of it, which had been brought by the wind, unlike the sterile cherry trees lining the streets."

"It had the sounds of a creek running behind it."

"It had wooden paneling in the bathroom and a bathtub with jets."

"It had tall windows the edges of which were painted with green."

"It had mice living inside the cutlery drawers."

And so on. She takes another cut.

Up the river a chemical plant is pouring out poisonous liquids downstream.

Her lungs fill with fluid, and as this occurs, she becomes aware of an asymmetry in the weight of her body.

The green dots appear through the pink dots, or is it the other way around, the pink dots appearing through the green dots?

She writes in her cloud notebook: "Describe the yard being cut."

One day the yard is cut down.

△   △
　△　△

The description moves through the object as it reaches it.

Bolts of fabric stand upright on a sidewalk, visible through a red square of occasion, like a theatre through which another theatre is visible: small puddles full of floating objects, cigarettes, sticks and plastic spoons.

The pigeons startle at the sound. And one pulls apart the orange brightness like a form of wool before the eyes.

In the articulate detail of sensation, not knowing when one experience is cut discrete as a floating particle, a person reaches with a stick into the puddle to look for cans. Blue flowers grow on a dividing line between the street and itself. A netting or a web shimmers in the wind. Materials are crude, embossed, a leopard print coat, a song.

Boxes of fresh ginger stacked in the sun on the street's interior, a drapery half hung to shield something. A black plastic bag breathing air into its belly.

On the twigs small orange berries among the flowers on sticks.

She writes in her cloud notebook: "This small, pink, slightly dirtied satin shoe sits in the window's interior."

The interiorities of seeing divide into dots, they are granular and discrete as if made out of some kind of enamel or stucco or melted candy that has hardened.

Something sits in this small pile, this ravine of thought, the waves of it and the passengers who imagine the waves as interiors.

Someone wears a dress, someone turns to the sky.

Seen this way from an aerial perspective they are free of narrative or striving, appearing only as an occurrence.

What becomes visible or manifest someday can never be properly hidden.

Any particular extent of space or surface, the dark areas in a painting, the dusty areas of a room.

This thing laces black with crisscrossing, the metal parts point in different directions, so many occasions in a grid.

There is a wish here for another realm, another dimension of the possible, a black lacquered table, a word pointing to a hand made out of letters, a plate of eggs, their yellow yolks shining.

All threads point in different directions.

An entrance occurs in the world's orbit.

△   △

△   △

They walk around the edges of consent.

"It is two thousand dollars in rent," she says, "and so we could never put it into the closing hand."

The privacy of any event is a handful, the sky is full of clouds and of the color blue, someone occasions themselves a seer and so the fabrics open to them. Lightness climbs a whole wall covered in a net. There are no visual occasions, only a coat's black, slick form as soft tissue and a gait.

Someone makes an interior called "Outdoor Voices."

And up in the air blue corroded scepters are held in the statues' hands. This is as close to the sky as anyone reaches, or it is between the sky and the ground where you are standing invisibly.

A pronoun is simply a latching of sensation in an increment. A rabbit made of sticks and small blue cups.

She writes in her cloud notebook: "What is the ground, oh what is the ground of inscription or the continent of its contents, a dispersion that will come as white flakes in the air."

She creates these defenses by studying one practice of labor against another.

Both are a graspable object.

Another understands redness, its stick form.

Something has crowded the stone into a thousand outward folds. The solid state one has listened to crickets in. Like a discrete form of history, the landscape returns these woven gifts.

The pigeons landing under each red awning at once, at once, and again.

The spray has landed on the walls, has made of the walls a surface.

The white bumps letting us know that we have reached the ground.

Something has fallen out of hand and not even upright glass tubes can contain it. Each of them a resting place, a winding blue string that divides perception from occurrence.

The plastics that she carries as eggs are scratched, hollow, but one cannot understand the shape of anything hollow without making inroads into it, and so of all ornaments and shapes of matter that are hollow or appear in this way.

$$\underline{\triangle} \quad \underline{\triangle}$$
$$\underline{\triangle} \quad \underline{\triangle}$$

Someone smells the shape of a princess and is turned away, or a copper wire is coiled and separated in the water, a ceramic blue mushroom grows in the alleyway.

The most likely unlikely pressings occur. And one leaps through the yellowed but translucent glass framed in the pink. Pink lick, lick pink, like a salt lick.

The blues stretching among the plants of different moments,

the window slightly cloudy with unwashed dust, powder blue as thought when rendered opaque to itself, visible.

The insides of books, not their colorful spines, face the outside of the world.

A green cap does not push anything out, the visibility of things a pile of material rearranging itself in the hands of capital.

Everyone here has the same hair, all the velvets and creased scarves, a kind of forgetting of pine needles in one's hand.

Not to wish this alien thing, a family of difference.

She speaks to the cut leaves, their branches on the ground, not looking where one sees.

The shopping breaks the surface of possible attention.

As all things when they are poured into the same opening, the same hole, their material difference becoming one malleability, inoffensive like melting blocks of soap or another sticky uniform substance.

She misses some relation to surface, a hallucination of grass following a displacement of attention.

A camel-colored object follows her. It has a hidden shape in it, as taped cardboard, or the maroon hairs licking another surface.

And then a third possibility appears.

She is not even making emotional copy for the capital's gnawing fingers.

A gaunt hanging thing with frizzles visible below a skirt or what are palm trees.

Or her murdered in the Puck building by a security guard, one of her shoes left there in a room.

She says, "don't leave my fingers, my thoughts there."

We take the same photograph standing next to each other. A piece of unoccupied ground, an open space.

△   △
 △   △

She gathers these yellow plums by the seashore.

The silk unwinds through the birches, the starlings in the sky, a posted clearing.

The voice dim, blue beetles milling, sitting, this slick thing behind you, behind the trees you cannot see a small blue tent in the woods, an enclosure only as big as your body, soap covering its surface.

The different moods or tones in the poem like different weather.

The leaping bodies of the deer invisible pressing sky continuing a description.

The description presses into the objects of which it seeks liquids or layers—marbles—all rock having been at some point a different kind of time, as all objects record inside them the impressions of other objects.

She writes in her cloud notebook: "The bourgeoisie cheerfully takes the impression of a host of objects. For slippers and pocket watches, thermometers and egg cups, cutlery and umbrellas it tries to get covers and cases. It prefers velvet and plush covers which preserve the impression of every touch."

The building makes a blue rim around its exterior, which winds into the cat's mouth pink — it lays the subjectivity there caught in small tones, a shining bell or modes of speech addressed to small things with fur.

Something cracks around the edges of speech, a blankness of what is for an instant unrecognizable but can be described as a shining, discarded thing under water, slowing down, mauve ribbon in hand or passing across a yellow line. Some other shapes open in sunlight. Another looks at the line coming through him or her, avoidant of fortune as seen exactly.

She says, "the yellow line is where the sun stops."

Someone places ornaments on the ground in order to attract some kind of animal.

The yellow rope, the color of mustard, is lost on the ground, or she wears a red string, a piece of red rope for protection.

One is divided between the impulse that is like hair on a pillow acting as cotton candy, some unknown range stretched and stretching there, a pass within the box that is the ribs, that is the voice, that is a heap of grain.

After someone leaves the fenced in rectangle on which they have fallen, the grass that they had seen and touched much earlier, the years dividing them from here and the blade that cuts their hair, the stone statues spray-painted red appear.

A waiting leans into a place from which a river is visible, the stone statues rising like ghosts as the curve in a landscape makes an intermittent passage through the lyric interiority of the object.

"What are statues but displaced figures," she thinks.

The sky appears and appears as a layer over everything that has disappeared.

She tries to take the photographs that the dead would have taken if they were not dead. They are of the sky, of the highway, of small blue eggs in a basket, the orange lights coming on over the exterior surfaces of factories, of empty parking lots, their white lines more visible in the failing light.

All time is this seeping of things.

It is possible for an array not to be able to register the appearance of something outside of it or just appearing there at its edges.

One could say that emotions are absent or present, although one could say that they are often present even though they are not always felt.

The backgrounds of things surprise us, it is like the woods seen simply as "the dark" or "space" behind other things in the landscape, and so small birds make cuts in and out of them invisibly.

A series of dots make an interest.

Encrustations or arrays can inhabit an interior, a hole dug in the ground away from direct contact with the sea, where the starfish and the anemones are brought for a moment to make an enclosed, inland sea.

$$\underline{\triangle \quad \triangle}$$
$$\underline{\triangle \quad \triangle}$$

One way to understand the movement in the grass is to think of a mouse.

It is winter though and the mouse may not be here.

"Placing a cactus outside in winter leads to death," she thinks.

"For the cactus, or the one who has placed it outside," they ask in unison.

A piece of wall may under certain conditions become indistinguishable from the side of a mountain, or a pink triangle made of wool may appear as a flush on someone's skin, the flight of pigeons from one brick building to another, or a whistle used to attract a horse.

Even when holding a thin piece of metal in one's hand, one may ask "is it copper, is it a bear, is it a cup?"

A flat neon light fixture in an office building may be replaced by a flat photograph of a fish on ice.

As she is walking home she imagines that all of the objects that had been made to stand like towers and sticks were made instead as excavations in the ground covered by starfish, sea anemones, and other forms of gem-like encrustations.

Someone tells her they are studying ancient sunlight, or how all the liquid or solid dark matter that has been burned over the past two hundred years has come from some sunlight, somewhere, touching something a long time ago.

She reads a story in which chitons are impregnated by men and then they die, not the chitons but the men die or wander off, while the chitons swell and winter and eventually birth a form of uncontainable difference.

Someone says, "when the sun sets in the world, the sun also sets in the poem," or is it the other way around, the poem having become wider and bigger than the world?

Someone else says, "a body is a paraphrase against a paper wall covered in violet flowers."

△   △

△   △

A wall is a gesture the grass moves across with relative quiet, a yellow rock entirely covered with lichen shines even in the dark as if on another planet.

A dress hangs on a chair depicting a small landscape: two boys, a mountain, a bird in the tree between them, or the mountain is a dune of pink seen through the fabric far away in the landscape, there and actual.

Some salt is shaken onto the surface of the table.

She does not remember whether the beetles had come out onto the streets late in the day or whether their appearance had occurred only at night.

She wishes to belong to a species that did it all at once, in a cloud of occurrence.

The smoothie fell apart not into liquid but into solid chunks of frozen strawberries, blobs of banana and other fruit-matter, a loose mixture floating in the background of a milky sea, now blue, now purple, as if a baby or another small animal had regurgitated its meal into her mouth. She felt that capitalism had failed her, the Magic Bullet had not made the objects of the world disappear into a homogenous mass that could transition seamlessly into the interiority of her body.

She considered the intransigence of the world, its refusal.

"What of the shapes that do not disappear," she thought, "that are still floating in the sea or sky."

The bridge was held up by the cement and blue steel, the wing was held up by muscle, the lines were held up by the asphalt beneath them, the voice was held up by ribbons of tissue, the mouth was held up by the teeth, a line of sight was held up by the telescope.

A tarp moved the color blue above the bed of a truck in movement also, the small horses appeared to move their bodies over the pink cloth, but what appeared as their movement was only a form of disappearance, some of their bodies visible here and now, and some later, with a delay.

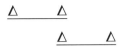

She listens to the sounds coming from the sky, the migrating geese making their triangle of sound stacked in rows, the bell-like croon of the raven. The sounds are unlike the sounds before them.

She walks along the windy island road reading about defenestration and begins to feel a thin, silver feeling in her hands as if of air passing.

She writes in her cloud notebook: "The snow covered the land in islands of white, we were surrounded by the water."

One night she turns off all the lights until the room is neon pink.

An owl appears in a dream, an owl appears in life and then flies off into the forest.

Rather than being a sign of one who has disappeared, she lies in a ditch on the side of the road where one figure changes into another, this time an unsexed figure into a figure of a woman.

She writes in her cloud notebook: "A plant in a bathroom grows toward the roll of toilet paper, and as it grows, its leaves begin to touch the paper, first the big flat leaf stroking its underside like a shelf and then the little leaf making a small roof or a window above it."

She spends the holiday inside a house shaped like a mushroom.

Moss can cover the surface of the roof in the way that the waves cover the sea or the sea covers the bottom on which it rests.

When seen from above it may appear to us as a miniature forest inside another forest.

The cows look at her and then approach with their ruddy red almost wild fur, making a row of waiting faces.

Or the gray and yellow chickens walk past her windows turning their heads this way, that way, their feathers puffed and distinct with arcs and dots in the winter air.

She considers the fullness of something like a cup or another kind of plenitude that can be held.

In her hand she carries a pink stone shaped like a cylinder with gray rectangular spots, like a speckled surface of an egg meant to hide it among the pebbles, in the moss or shrubs.

The smoke is carried from everything round and orange that is hanging from the trees.

What will occur inside the inner layer of the sun or another yellow shape drawn with a yellow pencil?

In the stream neon pink strands of aquatic grass move with the current, far away she still sees the light held in the wooded surfaces of things, small figures moving across them.

The day is a finitude of movement.

Vapors appearing from the enclosed rectangular shells or the white berries left attached on the twigs when the leaves retreat.

Each pattern is a story.

The visibility stirs, revealing the outlines of what is invisible, like the white posts of a soccer net without the netting or the fencing of a baseball diamond without the players.

The figure in a dream touching her is channeling another figure she cannot see.

A liquid translucency exits or layers a narrow space.

Dreaming is a space of dreaming, like white patches of snow left in the uneven shrubs.

In the blue distance ornaments of industry.

A flat movement or a passage beneath her like a sheet of thought or a thought's shadow, seeking in the flatness the upturned blue eggshells of discrete actions moving in the endless geometry of time.

"It is too blue," she says, "the mountains, the water, the sky."

$$\underline{\triangle} \quad \underline{\triangle}$$
$$\underline{\triangle} \quad \underline{\triangle}$$

In the thick of winter just other days.

A distance in something unraveling, as if she prevented herself from seeing it all at once—a disappearing peach or another fruit left in a closed wooden box, where it could be viewed only through a magnifying lens, which also distorts it.

A tree had grown toward the ground instead of growing toward the sky.

Red sand in a cup.

In a book the color of roses she reads about "delicate empiricism" and considers the way that relation is generative of the objects of sensation.

One day she is hired to help navigate the tensions between dog walkers and bird watchers in a large city park.

The wood has a rose-pink glow inside it she does not entirely understand.

A side of leaning pink glass through which pigeons are visible and beyond them trees.

A small flight of something cold occurs in the detail between the bricks.

In the air something draws yellow lines.

She walks to the river to see.

Or in the leaning green sea of the blanket the pigeons are pecking.

The mountain today divides itself into snow, green cloud, and light.

If a texture is set at a right scale of proportion, all perception can occur within its openings.

Think of pink sugar then as cotton candy or a pink lion drawn in chalk, the snow having landed on the tops of trees.

She writes in her cloud notebook: "The tops of trees covered in snow like a brushed surface changing."

On a beach someone stands holding a jar in which a changing thing—a ctenophore—flickers jello-like, or a poodle sits on a sofa next to a painted portrait of itself, its background pink and purple streaks of color.

To watch something changing, to really see its bright edge, the events occurring inside it, is to notice detail appear in the crevices of green where no detail was visible before: through a microscope even a fly's wing is a frolic of golden lines and pink openings.

One can also think of everything that would have appeared if something had not disappeared.

△   △
  △   △

The pink enters the sky because the sky is like any other object and can be entered or closed.

In the blue sheets.

Or the blue is something leaning that can be held up by the bricks on the leaning frame of wood.

Or the sky is something drawn in gold pencil on a sheet of thin paper each day.

Or in her cloud notebook she writes "the sky" above a golden rectangle.

When the sky clears, the mountains appear closer and bigger and more blue, a heavier kind of blue than the blue of the truck seen through the fence holding the last threads, sheets, or increments of light.

Or the sky is in the inverse of the moving slick on the pool of water, filled with the dead plants of winter, a long, stretched thing rimmed in red.

Or the small holes appear in the bark, like worms.

She writes in her cloud notebook: "The gold nuggets fell out of the cavities and landed in the dirt. The dirt was continuous like one long sheet. Sometimes it found forms of difference or separation in the long stomachs of worms. Anything contains an outside inside of it. A doughnut is a simple shape with a hole. They had entered the interior of the office building, moving through the dim corridor toward the red light."

The sky, as what moves between the trees, high in their branches, or the sheen of their insides, the sky passing to the invisible here, the thought in sheets lifted at golden joints.

Oh, to make a latch that is neither a closure nor an opening, but a doodle, something laying in sheets, the pink appearing around it like a rim.

The rats shift in relation to those who had caught them.

They are scents in the blue of the night, some transmission in the wet air, a sheet of silver.

The oranges appear or the cubes of sugar in cups, that is of the dead, the slits of sky as something cut in gold metal, quills filled with dust as banks, something in a dream turns a card and she turns away from the body, callouses form on the edges of objects.

She writes in her cloud notebook: "The worms were in love with the nuggets of gold and so they forgot about the continuities of the dirt and the inner cavities of their bodies. The worms said "lick, lick, click, click" and the gold said "click, click, lick, click."

Or the birds set wild fires in the grasses so that the rodents can run out into the open field, appear, and the birds can come and feast upon them.

In a dream, a sheet of orange opens and then divides into small windows of orange. The windows are small pieces of fish draped over something.

A sparrow appears, or she writes to Sparrow about the weather on the other side of the continent, the weather appears as something occurring in a movie.

They have placed small sheets of blue fabric over the windows to simulate the sky.

Or the roof is made out of straw, its billowing pillows contained in plastic bags and red tape. If this were a story called "Three

Little Pigs," the house would be blown away by now.

In the great wind the window breaks, someone invisible knocking on the other side of it, the edge of their orange helmet visible, the logo covered with silver duct tape. "Does every window contain a history of all of its knockings?" she asks.

In the wind they think of the body, but the body is already gone, the soft layers of shirts around its neck, and then she invites it in, but it does not appear, the sheets of the window glass knocking in the wind through the feeling that had appeared inside the body on the porch.

She sits in a room with pink walls, rimmed in white plaster rectangles of flowers. She does not know then if the body still exists, she sees it in different forms of disappearing. "Is disappearing a form?" she asks then.

△   △
△   △

She says, "yes, we were on the floor of the plane"; she says, "yes, it was dark"; she says, "yes, we were sitting on wooden boards pressed against each other and weeping at nothing visible."

Sometimes one must enter a space to exit another larger one, and so of a small fish that had been painted with iridescence from a thousand fish scales held there all at once in their smaller, more minute forms.

The sunlight leaves.

A shape exits a form of itself that it had held for a moment a few moments ago, and so of a color green that passes across the side of a mountain, intermittently there where the clouds are not.

The strawberries embedded in the cake squished into its sponginess, bleeding a little across that margin between them and the cake, disappearing or leaving a red rim where something else had been.

She writes in her cloud notebook: "I remember that in summer time I once left by chance a cut lemon in a close room, and two months afterwards I found a putrefaction growing on the cut part, tufts of hair an inch high at least, and on the top of each hair a kind of head, like the head of a small snail, plainly beginning to imitate a plant."

A permission is given for objects to populate a world, for instance, this t-shirt the color of a cantaloupe, which had at one time formed a ceiling, its arc or dome, or the bottom of a red drawer, which had at one time contained comic books and the sea.

What war renders invisible—displaces—must continue to

be seen, a geography does not pass in time but adds itself to another, as another time in another place.

A forest can be counted, although should it be counted from the inside or from the outside?

A cloth can be turned to reveal three figures walking.

She considers the silks in her hands as a way of addressing herself to color. "All that is seen enters the sun," she thinks, "and even those shapes that pass through the hands are held there only for a moment."

From the deck of a ship she sees stars, or is it the other way around, the surface of a ship cast into the sky, where its hull moves among other objects.

All that appears in any hand appears in each hand.

A small light is held in a green glass bowl, or is it the water that had appeared between the ships?

Inside each tree another tree, and then another inside that one, and then another, etc.

Or those who had formed a mosaic of green tiles on the ground as a way of presenting a flower or a hand, a sky or a bird.

She considers then whether the sky can be thought such a shape, its thickness not visible.

In movement, another movement—as in a bird moving through the sky.

She considers the smallest possible distance between objects that can still be seen.

If the weight of two objects, a red cube positioned on the surface of the table and the blue cube next to it, differs by only ten grams, it can be felt, but only if the objects themselves are quite light, below a certain proportion of the weight that holds a difference between them.

"Is touch a form of speech," she thinks again, "and if yes, how can it be distinguished from ways of speaking, or if it cannot, what of the promiscuities that occur each time that language is used?"

It is this other mode of movement that she wants to count among things.

They go to view the sky even though the sky cannot be seen, something else smells of lemons, or the crushed vertices of objects held there, a translucent fish with orange and black spots passes beneath, the body full of its repetitions or broken into them until no difference is left, no translucent edges around the objects of time.

Each window that opens into sensation.

Or the leaves that open in the stacking of a cavity.

She thinks of the windows that open in time, the apples ripening in a poem or a clear orb that passes within the thin tubes tying onto another enclosure.

What is written in their shapes as they are changing, these ostensibly still things that can be viewed.

She comes to view them as if to remember their distance.

Or a stranger places overripe bananas and mangos, pears, by the side of the road where a cairn sits, to mark it where it had come to rest.

"Although, how can an invisibility be marked in space," she thinks, "when it can only be known by its absence."

They ask if the birds had moved the rocks, and no one answers.

She tries to press a translucent shape around all objects moving in time, attempting to delineate them from one another as if parsing words.

She writes in her cloud notebook: "I am putting makeup on empty space / all patinas convening on empty space / rouge blushing on empty space / I am putting makeup on empty space / pasting eyelashes on empty space / painting the eyebrows of empty space / piling creams on empty space / painting the phenomenal world / I am hanging ornaments on empty space / gold clips, lacquer combs, plastic hairpins on empty space."

She writes in her cloud notebook: "Now the landscape changes, the pink enters it, the seagulls come to rest on the red roof, time slows down inside the encrustations of objects."

She thinks of the other woman living in the apartment building across the way, the way here being a slope or a body of water.

"What does it mean to write from a displaced position," she asks.

Her, or the other woman, as if carrying a displacement of water inside herself, has fallen out of the tub when the other object had fallen in.

This is where she had found the ground, or this is where she had found the sky.

"What is an orbit but a shelter," she asks.

△ △
△ △

She considers the relationship between imminence and description, or if everything appearing were to be seen.

She thinks of the empiricism of fine glitter she has placed on one of her fingers or the birds gathering above the sea, each one a hologram of an oval opening in space.

If the right kinds of fronds or tentacles, scraps or leftovers, tissues or dangles were to be attached around the rim of such an opening, they would act as an additive surface, making more ways of touch possible.

Or they would act as a filter, a precise latch.

Perhaps texture is what cannot be met.

It appears as a plaque or a plaque is wiped until it has no discernible shape.

Wanting milk and standing.

Looking at the sky.

Some cannot align everything that pulls inside them with all of the elastic things positioned in the world.

She writes of the air—how it is neither on the inside nor on the outside but supports something in the realm of bone and muscle, the realm of the sky.

Does a shape have a pink liquid coming out of it—so mobile it can act as a receiver—a sticky substance in which words can linger in that confusion between touch and knowledge.

She only watches the ones where their faces can't be seen, even when he says, "look at the camera."

So much is mobile, the green rope that had been on the ground a week before and then broke apart into smaller discernible threads is now gone, the wolves have exited the forest. One afternoon sitting in the sun she tells the whole story, how she went into the mountain with the apple salesman, how later she spoke to birds saying "why are you sitting here on someone else's land, čuč," how another hid a baby in a room during the war while the others walked through the forest, how a horse carried a child from a train, how they were pushed onto buses with two suitcases, how she switched their coffees in case one of them was poisoned, how she said that something would shut down inside her if she had to deal with loneliness again.

Beneath all of the artworks in which the sky is framed.

He says, "inside each object, there is a form of duration."

That survives winter.

△　　△
　△　　△

She writes in her cloud notebook: "At one time these blackberry bushes held our thoughts in their hands, in their thorns rather, seeing as though blackberry bushes have no such parts as hands and possess the other instead."

She writes in her cloud notebook: "One figure climbed down into the ravine to pick the berries, the other stood on the path reading *The Maximus Poems* out loud. The first wore a cowboy shirt with red and silver embroidery on the lapels and carried a yogurt cup to place the blackberries into. The second waited. The sounds of the moving river came up from the bottom of the ravine."

"How small can a story be if lizards have to fit into it?" she asks.

A white diamond appears between the trees.

A city in which an action is simply to stand and look at the mountains.

A rare green appearing in them, between the clouds, or all smoke and vapor becoming one connected moving surface across a rectangle of space in which everything appears each day differently; the same can be said of the sky or any open surface on which occasions occur.

She thinks about all temporalities of waiting: the caterpillar waiting for the buds to turn into leaves, the flowers waiting for the bees, all forms of waiting that have appeared in women, those waiting in lines for water, those waiting for permission to stay.

At the scene of the accident the grass looks just like grass by the side of any highway, the small green trees that do not become the forest that do not recede into anything, the same ordinary even light blue sky.

She tries to discern a difference in the photograph between this place and anywhere else, but the surface remains closed to her, empirical and exact.

She hears sea birds in the distance, she sees seashells by the seashore.

Between the fingers there is always a space through which birds can pass.

The soft orange body that had been the sea, that had been the box, that had been the hovering sky, that had been the insertion, comes apart.

She sees the small goats that had been born the night before but this does not restore her faith in the continuity of things appearing and disappearing.

Shadows subtract themselves from things, or in each thing an uneven movement of light and something other: it is the weight of the water held back by the dam that makes it move forward.

She sits in a moment of knowing on a porch, and then she tries to sit inside of that moment again and again.

The figure next to her says, "I feel this in my body."

All happiness is just a color among other streaks of color, she thinks.

"Can't we stay here?" she asks, but the shape next to her is singing a song without an arrival.

△   △

△   △

She writes in her cloud notebook: "You are the last / Who will know him / Nurse. // Not know him, / He is an old man, / A patient, / How could one know him? // You are the last / Who will see him / Or touch him, / Nurse."

Some lights visible through the moving trees indicate the presence of others, of felt space moving outward from varying points of perspective.

She had always wanted to see across that sea to a version of herself appearing, not on the inside of her body but as a point of perspective in the landscape.

A corduroy cloth covered with blue birds and outside of the bird's cages filled with other birds (this time blue and yellow), a red rabbit and an upside-down fawn.

The objects intercept what is narrative in the world's appearing, or maybe it is the other way around, the objects being like small suns out of which narrative can radiate.

She writes in her cloud notebook: "The poem records the edge of the world within itself. The trees on the outside of the forest feel the world differently. The goldfish shimmer differently at the edges of a group."

She writes in her cloud notebook: "A shape may release another shape beside it to act as decoy, the first shape being made out of flesh, and the other of an inky liquid dissolved in another liquid."

The blue sofa sits inside the room, on the outside of the room are the trees and the sky.

She thinks of the interior rooms of intention—their pink wallpaper—but does not wish to describe them: it is between their orbits and what appears corporeal that change occurs.

The small moons arriving over the surface of the planets.

Or grain left to soak in a bowl overnight, its small orbs making for even smaller planets.

She gets off at cherry street or the ground is covered by the colors that preceded the appearance of cherries.

Description can be indirect so as to leave its object behind within a halo of subtraction. In this way it becomes indiscernible whether the object had preceded the description at all.

Something can be described as an opposition when it may simply be a blue rectangle around another shape.

An address could be a place to come to in the night.

A horse moves around his pasture in a rectangular shape so that it is not clear whether it is the ground that is the delimitation of the shape of movement or whether it is the figure that makes the shape visible.

Likewise it is unclear when silk cloth is embroidered with silk thread what is the medium or the message.

Someone whispers to her about a silk television she cannot see.

Something makes a sentence that twists and turns like a helical shape that is forming.

The doughnuts covered with holiday sprinkles on a billboard

are bigger than her body, bigger by several orders of magnitude.

She calls someone on the phone heading into a city that contains a room lit in pink neon with messages scrawled on the walls and says: "I am on a bridge."

The foxes playing on the tent's surface make all kinds of shadows and the shadows turn into voices.

She writes in her cloud notebook: "I see you so clearly, even though you are not seen any more."

She writes in her cloud notebook: "The boys are gemlike."

She writes in her cloud notebook: "It's not liquid, it's not substantial."

She writes in her cloud notebook: "The ethics of the dust: mineralogy as subject formation."

She writes in her cloud notebook: "The marble answer is in its rimmed shape."

She writes in her cloud notebook: "Smoke cedar ice cream."

"What is it for you to touch someone," she wants to ask, "is it a finding of something that does not yet exist or always the traversal of the same devoid surface?"

"Neither," the gendered person says, avoiding the occasion of gender.

△   △

△   △

A blue canoe tied down with pink rope upside down.

The infinite detail of the flowers that had appeared even on just that one tree, not flowers but some kind of inflorescence that appears before the leaves, more like a set of threads in the air, pink and yellow, a change in tone seen from above as if a field had opened slightly red, almost blue, a window of time entering an object in which it can receive an arrival of change.

Or all convolutions seen from above are non-narrative.

She thinks about inscape and what cuts off the edges of perception / makes their shards.

Two women pet a dog.

A man with a green light behind a black screen puts pieces of metal together with what we know is fire but looks at the moment more like limes.

Or this sounds like fabric.

The walls of the white building with holes cut out of them so that something can exit as something else passes through.

△   △

　△   △

Yellow glass, like a form of honey suspended in air, marks one surface where another surface was held in its absence, a desert rose shawl wraps around a shape, upright is the sky.

They say 6,000 small bodies could make a silk tent for those in movement, the movement underneath them slipping, rearranging time and space even when they have stopped moving.

In a desert, or what had not been a desert before, a man stands manufacturing smaller more delicate deserts out of blue tarp and sticks, these smaller more delicate deserts pooling to stop the spread of the larger desert around them.

She stands in a specific pool of sunlight or holds a lamp where the sunlight had been.

Someone watches for the appearance of plants.

Across one window of the circle a worm enters and crosses a time window in which a leaf appears.

"You walk right in the window of the sky," a man says on the street to no one in particular.

She walks so slowly, threads drop behind her.

Or birds fly in and out of the sky's opening, a blue door.

The fantasies that interest us may be precut or cut as an alignment of shapes into which a hand can be placed.

You say, "I have surrounded myself with the shapes of plants," or, beyond the blue opening, droplets of slight minerals in a dissolved set of orbits mark the surface of the hand with tinctures.

The smell of laundry is something that may be considered a living form, a singular recorded shape / also wood cast in light, a ceramic cup with a set of waves written on it.

To move without purpose just to cast to be cast in light—a red embroidery on a shirt of flowers and green leaves, on a building that may sit on another seaside, even though it is here coincident.

Blue eggs left, their edges translucent boundaries in a moving geometry of time.

"The tree greens" or "the tree is blueing" somewhere at the boundary with the sky.

Each of them "blueing" in particular without being visible to the others.

"What if each object were wrapped in mist that would make it unfold from the present into a different future?" you ask.

"Subjectivity is distributed like rose chalk, small and particulate," she says.

The final sun crosses the buildings, finds its outlines in the dust. Fragmentation is a zero form, those trees which into the sky send occasions, the yellow painted around a door—there is a promise of shining light to the lapsed things, this composed square of sound, the moving leaves.

A poem is just an outline around thought that cannot be avoided.

The words do not carry the weight of yellow flowers or a stained silence in the oil, but sensation is in the instruments of sensation unamplified.

The name is deictic, or it acts as a replacement for what is possible, what cannot be let out.

Somehow one reaches for time, that first form of light cast between things—the red curtains, the pyramid, or the scratches a kitten makes on your hands.

We list the forms of alignment, but they are not synchronous; she carries the metal of one coast on one hand and that of the other on the other.

"Please do not pick the flowers," the man says to his small child (something you would not have said), the yellow suspended like honey in a glass.

"The sound is the invisible thing," you say.

"Your doll is so beautiful even if you don't see it."

So many possible outward forms, each one wanting to sit still as it is touched.

This thing that occurs, the purple appearing inside of things, an outside at the edges of the orbit into which the planet enters.

How to distribute the particles so that there is maximum relation between them?

You are again with a cup in which a sugar cube is dissolving and there is no spoon, just a pattern of waiting.

One waiting for the lattice of the other outline inside it, adjusts it—its circular silver orbit without voice.

In an Uber a man asks if her name means "island" and she says "yes."

$$\underline{\triangle \quad \triangle}$$
$$\underline{\triangle \quad \triangle}$$

I tell her of red flags, how any object has many unused directions in it.

It is a practice of lines having wanted to be visual, or as if the task were to endlessly tell of the ground, its perception.

A red insect drips onto the paper and something surrounds it.

Thought can make anything into a thousand blue lines.

Or one cannot know the whole population of tiny figures that live on the inside of a leaf or what the island is when it is cut in two.

A subtle weight, as when you pick up a red cube from the table and can tell its just perceptible difference, or the orb of the sun, which you forget is a circle.

The figures you point to in the world of geometry, a swimming pool, winter, and what is visible in this sense of displacement.

You hear of the separations and see the girl who is standing.

The vision is toward you, even when you appear to be looking out.

An object is also a self.

Beneath a blue fence someone has drawn hills with black lines or scrawled in all caps on the side of a truck: "RABBIT MOVERS."

You think of the rabbits moving, but moving what? Or, the

quality of rabbits, their slick weight, fur like glass or a faraway liquid, the animals appearing to you on the grass as a sign.

Each area could be where sailors used to come with their dream of land.

A poem is something malleable like a membrane that encloses perception, where objects always come to land in what is sensed, a long evening.

The girl is still standing, maybe next to a bus, you cannot see her or the waiting that surrounds her.

Once a cut is made, it is made again, like editing a film where a sign of birds or a boat can make a reoccurrence, but also where the uncontainable sits like long stalks of grass.

You learn to think of yourself as the ground of inward and outward geometries, their red vertices a thin web of insects, like a song.

Or we make the length of evening into a line, its granularity of detail like what a snail sees in the enormity of leaves you walk inside of to take a photograph.

On the other side of the world someone says something you

have once said about the movement of starfish on the sea floor, how it may appear fast when it is slow or how slow it is even when it appears fast.

Or if you look carefully at the trees, there is always infinite movement between the sparrows.

The red plaid shirt is as if drawn with pink chalk, in that it could turn into a slow cloud or disperse into the impermanence that marks the edges of all objects. The travelers touching the marble hands carry them away as atoms clinging to their human hands and then clinging to the world.

Narrative makes small latches in all objects, so that something is refigured by a set of marks on its surface, carrying in it everything that it has touched, changed by this, even as it also contains its own invisible change.

A pink edge on purple or red shorts.

A smear in the hill's orbit.

Above, the birds could be falling out of flight.

The enclosure of yellow like sugar.

The moment held at the top of the stairs, before the second dog descends.

In an invisible situation someone holds your hand.

Yellow is visible on the quiet water.

Or a pink lake encrusted in crystals moving its shape.

A hollow cut out of the snow.

How thin is the thread on which an image can alight before it falls, the ripped black threads of her shorts hanging in space, or a film being shown on a piece of cloth?

One of the skies closes.

△   △
    △   △

What is an investigation in narrative, as if someone placed its smallest moments as tiny cubes on the surface of the table without telling the edges of time apart from the edges of space.

Or the blue-legged birds nesting on a rock go out to the sea to fish, but as the temperatures rise, the fish move into deeper water, so the edge texture at which they used to meet—the convex line of the dive and the concave line of surfacing—is a site of unmeeting.

Or on the underside of the blue fence the paint has clustered into a thousand hardened drips, like ripples of an upside-down sea of waiting.

"Why is there a red light on your dress now?"

The blue shutters open to an enclosure, its face a thousand red moving dots, berries on winter trees or ladybugs running over the remembered shape of a body having been taken apart, the white dust in the sea or a reservoir held back by the stones. Someone knows how below the long hair sweat had gathered, wood, the tasks of windows on a blue house.

A large rock, almost black, with jagged surfaces, covered with a plethora of silver dots.

The winter scene seen through a small bathroom window disturbs because it has no mood attached to it, it falls out of mood. It is then that the night sky falls out of things too. That second moment, looking at the night sky, and nothing occurs in it. It is devoid of a cosmology, or it does not sit within or evoke an order.

What we're seeing is only one of the device's "classical configurations," she says. "But somewhere, not perceived by us right now, there are other versions." According to her, this is true not just for tape recorders but all physical objects. "Even for systems like you and me," she says. "There is a different configuration of all of us in a parallel universe."

All histories arise out of touch.

Trying to not create these endless negative eggshells, which require infinite things to fill them, and hence always register the failing point in every relation.

In this scene a girl rearranges all of the objects in a room. She eventually pulls the mattress out of its frame and places it on the floor. Everything else, including the bed frame and other furniture is discarded. She sits and begins writing while kneeling on the mattress that is on the floor. Sometimes, while she is writing on the floor, she eats sugar with a spoon out of a half-full bag of sugar next to her.

The figures sit outside a white mesh cage, not a soft cage, but a hard one that you would see sheltering a small animal like a hedgehog at an old zoo.

The poem can be turned upside down, like flipping the skirts (so that the little girl is also the wolf, so that grandma is also the little girl, so that the wolf is also the grandma, and so on, ad infinutum).

The forest is also the time that occurs in a bubble sailing across the wind's back before it enters it.

She can feel my temperature rising, it feels like yellow locum cubes covered in white sugar.

Sometimes these are called Turkish Delights.

In the upper echelons of the cone of memory something dislodges, like floaters moving in the film of perception.

The film of perception is wet.

The precipice whiteness of birch trees cannot be said.

Something long in the snow makes its registration or language finds such things as a thread of appearing sky / the blue ropes stretched in the snow.

△   △
 △   △

Language of preference can be used as a veiled threat.

Water on the surface of things can appear as a medium or a molecule can appear as a surface of touch.

Some sheets of cloth resolve into smooth fibers even under magnification, some are coarse, unbelievable, like the surface of the moon.

She is carried first, then she changes size.

When dropped in water, this compound dissolves.

Off to the side the juice has stained the surface of the paper three times, or is it cloth that her hand is wrapped in moving into and against her face.

To stand against this language, she thinks of weaving through the thin passes of green water, being invisible inside the color of it until she strikes, wanting to preserve that invisible softness that occurs before the strike.

Not all of this is smoothness, she thinks: the cow has a big mouthful of grass in her big mouth.

Later, there in the yard, the animals uncover the parts that she has buried.

What returns is the wooden stem that had been attached to the orange.

Without seeing the body she does not know what was visible of it, what invisible, what they could hold in their hands or would have wanted to.

In not knowing something closely, one may not know how to touch it, this is as true of the dead as it is of cats who may not wish to be stroked backwards.

Sometimes everything of the world is made up of rectangular Ziploc bags filled with pink bubble wrap that one may be permitted to carry into an airport to contain small bottles of shampoo.

Each of these is a small act of change: the rats were petted, stroked, flecked, their ears were touched, their noses sniffed and rubbed and licked, and that is how they were made to change, to change with those who had rubbed, petted, flecked, and stroked them.

This is the twenty-third bowl.

Not all the sand of the world could ever be carried.

Nor divided in half.

Each of the hairs in the brush came from somewhere.

She thinks of the uncountable, the unconstrained.

She writes in her cloud notebook: "Hans the horse could not do math but he could read the unconscious surfaces of bodies."

She writes in her cloud notebook: "The world changed until it was full of bears and wolves and possums and hedgehogs and worms and eyes and cats and beetles, and those things without eyes."

This was the sea urchin republic.

No one arrived here.

Acknowledgments

This book often blurs the distinction between direct citation and oblique reference, but in these different ways it is in dialogue with Theresa Hak Kyung Cha's texts *Dictee*, "object/subject," and "Personal Statement and Outline of Postdoctoral Project"; Tan Lin's *Seven Controlled Vocabularies and Obituary 2004: The Joy of Cooking*; Jakob von Uexküll's *A Foray into the Worlds of Animals and Humans* and "An Introduction to Umwelt"; Aida Begić's film *Snijeg (Snow)*; Gertrude Stein's play *He Said It. Monologue*, her lectures "Poetry and Grammar" and "Plays," as well as *The Geographical History of America* and "Sentences"; a class on moss I took at the University of British Columbia in 2004; stories told about the Bosnian war by those in my family who survived it, including my father Esad Smailbegović, who spent more than three years in Sarajevo under siege, and my mother Azra Ramadanović, who escaped the city in the middle of the war to find me so that we could be refugees together in Rijeka, Croatia; Robert Hooke's *Micrographia*; Karen Barad's *Meeting the Universe Halfway*; RISD Nature Lab; Leibniz's *Monadology*; Lucretius' *De rerum natura*; Francesca Woodman's photographs and her book *Some Disordered Interior Geometries*; Rosemary Mayer's artworks and her exhibition at the Swiss Institute, New York, in 2021; Dorothy Wordsworth's journals; Chantal Akerman's film *Je tu il elle*; Andrei Tarkovsky's films *Stalker* and *Mirror*; Marian Engel's *Bear*; Mei-mei Berssenbrugge's *Four Year Old Girl* and her concept of "delicate empiricism"; the American Museum of Natural History's gem collection; William James's *The Principles of Psychology*; Hieronymus Bosch's paintings; Caitlin Hurst's capacity for recognizing "strange speech" and for the gift of the initial cloud notebook; Matthew Thurber for helping me develop a drawing practice and for rerouting the ants away from the honey; thistles bought at Trader Joe's with Leah Pires in May 2020 and the journey north after; Leslie Marmon Silko's *Ceremony*; *8. Mart u Ratu, Sarajevo 8.3.93 (March 8th in War, Sarajevo 8.3.93)*, a video by Daniela Gogić, Oliver Todorović, Ahmed Imamović, Almir Kenović, and Srđan Vuletić; The Cat Practice; Willy Kühne's optograms of the rabbit's retina; Mark Baumer throwing the cherries in Whyte Lake; ceiling carpet at Bethel Acupuncture; Benjamin